FIRST A COMMENTARY FOR TODAY
CORINTHIANS

for
Cynthia

FIRST CORINTHIANS
A COMMENTARY FOR TODAY

William A. Beardslee

Chalice Press
St. Louis, Missouri

Cover design: Bob Watkins
Art Director: Michael Dominguez

10 9 8 7 6 5 4 3 2 1

Library of Congress Cataloging–in–Publication Data

Beardslee, William A.
    First Corinthians : a commentary for today / William A. Beardslee.
        p.   cm.
    Includes bibliographical references.
    ISBN 0-8272-1018-3
        1. Bible. N.T. Corinthians, 1st—Commentaries.   I. Title.   II. Title:
    1 Corinthians   III. Title : 1st Corinthians.
    BS2675.2.B43 1994   94-27009
    227'.207—dc20   CIP

Printed in the United States of America

Contents

INTRODUCTION

The Challenge of 1 Corinthians	1
Listening to Paul/Listening to the Corinthians	2
The City and the Church	3
The Occasion for 1 Corinthians	4
The Form of 1 Corinthians	6
The Outline and Unity of 1 Corinthians	8
Faith and Its Ethical Application	10
Radical Transformation and Continuing Responsibility	11
Self-consciousness and Love	13
Then and Now: Different Problems and a Common Quest	15

COMMENTARY

1:1–9 INTRODUCTION: GREETING AND THANKSGIVING	19
1:10—4:21 THE "BODY" OF THE LETTER: DIVISIONS IN THE CHURCH AND WISDOM MISUNDERSTOOD	22
1:10–17 Divisions in the Church	24
1:18–31 From Practical Behavior to Basic Faith	25
2:1–16 Wisdom and Foolishness	28
3:1–23 Missing the Point: What Paul, Apollos, and the Others Were About	30
4:1–21 The Challenge to Paul's Authority	32
Preaching and Teaching on 1 Corinthians 1—4	34
5:1—11:1 FIRST MAIN SECTION OF "SPECIFIC ISSUES": QUESTIONS OF PERSONAL BEHAVIOR IN THE COMMUNITY	46
5:1–13 A Community Defiled by Violation of a Taboo	47
Preaching and Teaching on 1 Corinthians 5	53
6:1–20 Two Issues That Test the Community: Litigation and Wrong Sexual Behavior	56

Preaching and Teaching on 1 Corinthians 6 61
7:1–40 Marriage and the Roles of Men and Women 62
Preaching and Teaching on 1 Corinthians 7 74
8:1—11:1 Love and Knowledge in Conflict Over the
  Question of Food Sacrificed to Idols 79
  8:1–13 Love and Knowledge 83
  9:1–27 Paul's Own Practice as an Example of Setting
    One's Own Claims Aside 86
  10:1–13 The Threat of Idolatry: An Example from
    the Past 92
  10:14–22 Participation in the Lord's Supper 95
  10:23—11:1 Freedom and Consideration Once Again 97
  Preaching and Teaching on 1 Corinthians 8:1—11:1 98

11:2—14:40 SECOND MAIN SECTION OF "SPECIFIC
ISSUES": ISSUES IN THE CONDUCT OF WORSHIP 103
  11:2–16 The Proper Appearance of Women (and Men) Who
    Speak in Worship 104
  11:17–34 Danger in the Lord's Supper 108
  Preaching and Teaching on 1 Corinthians 11 111
  12:1–31a Diversity of Gifts and One Spirit 114
  Preaching and Teaching on 1 Corinthians 12 119
  12:31b—13:13 Love as the Highest Gift 121
  Preaching and Teaching on 1 Corinthians 13 129
  14:1–40 Being Carried Beyond Oneself *versus*
    Understanding and Sharing 133
  Preaching and Teaching on 1 Corinthians 14 140

15:1–58 THIRD MAIN SECTION OF "SPECIFIC ISSUES":
THE RESURRECTION 143
  Preaching and Teaching on 1 Corinthians 15 150

16:1–24 THE COLLECTION, TRAVEL PLANS,
EXHORTATIONS, AND GREETINGS 158
  Preaching and Teaching on 1 Corinthians 16 161

WORKS CITED 163

INDEX OF PRINCIPAL THEMES 167

Preface

This book has been written for the general reader, and with an eye to bringing this powerful letter into the life of faith and action that we live today.

Those who know the books written about 1 Corinthians will recognize which ones I have drawn upon for the interpretations offered here—though some of these interpretations are not drawn from books. I have not tried to indicate these sources or to give proper scholarly credit. This was not easy to do, for a lifetime of training has inclined me to full footnote references. However, in order not to distract from the letter itself and the ways of reading it that are suggested here, references have been kept to a minimum.

I will have to say that none of the many books I consulted surpasses, in interest and stimulation, Johannes Weiss's *Der erste Korintherbrief*, published in 1910 and, unfortunately, never translated from German. Of the more recent literature, I have learned the most, and I have had my thinking changed the most, by several works by women scholars. Most writers on 1 Corinthians have assumed that the interpreter's task is to understand Paul against the background of the defective Corinthians. In contrast, these more recent scholars see that the letter has to be interpreted in a setting of give and take, of mutual learning where not all the right is on one side. I know that some of them will think that I should have listened to them with even greater attention. Three of these works are listed in the Works Cited.

From time to time a few books are mentioned, so that an interested reader can follow up on a suggestion or line of thought proposed here, and can discover what a full-fledged scholarly interpretation, or a theological exploration, is like. These are samples only, though important ones. Their authors and titles are given in the text, and full references will be found in the Works Cited, at the end of this volume.

Many people as well as books have contributed to my thinking about this important letter. In particular I am grateful to Paul Achtemeier for reading parts of the manuscript, to Kristin Mann for help in setting the conflict of chapter 5 in a wider setting, and especially to William Baird for a careful reading of the whole manuscript and for insightful criticisms. I thank David P. Polk and Chalice Press for publishing this study of 1 Corinthians.

Unless otherwise indicated, quotations from the Bible are given in the New Revised Standard Version. (See the abbreviations below for a full list of the translations quoted.)

I have dedicated this book to my wife, Cynthia. In the six years of our marriage I have learned profoundly from her about the nature of a fellowship that is truly open to all sorts of people—a major theme of 1 Corinthians.

Abbreviations

KJV—King James Version
RSV—Revised Standard Version
NEB—New English Bible
TEV—Today's English Version

Introduction

The Challenge of 1 Corinthians

First Corinthians contains some of the best-known sections of the Christian Bible, especially its chapter 13 on love and chapter 15 on the resurrection. Yet the power of the book may easily elude us; so much of it deals with the concrete problems of an ancient church that we may find it hard to see how the words of Paul are speaking to us. This gap between "then" and "now" is not really very different from what we face in reading any book of the Bible, but in 1 Corinthians we become aware of it and cannot escape it.

We shall have to know something about that ancient church and about the ways in which people spoke and wrote about faith in those days if we are to understand the letter. But the real challenge of 1 Corinthians lies at another point. It is precisely because it is so fully a real letter—a specific response to a series of concrete problems—that it opens for us so powerful a picture of faith as a journey, rather than as a static state. The eternal love of God was made concrete for Paul in Christ, and to speak of this he drew abundantly from the forms of speech of the time. But it is not the antiquity of these forms that we need to focus on. Rather, as we think about the interplay between the "then" and the "now," we may become more aware that our own engagement with the letter opens us to further stages of our own journey.

Paul was dealing with concrete issues; some of these we no longer face, and others we face in different form. In the process Paul was trying to clarify what faith and Christ are. This letter

1

was only one step in the process. The task of interpretation will rightly focus on this interplay between the concrete circumstances (which, then as now, keep changing) and the lure of God to deal creatively with the circumstances and find a direction for our responses.

It has been a constant temptation for Christians to think that they have grasped the eternal in the words of their Scripture, their confession, or their theology. It would be wiser instead to say that these words report a profound search for and a profound response to the call of God. First Corinthians is a basic document, perhaps *the* basic document, in the Bible that helps us see this. We shall confront our own responsibility as readers as we interpret it. The letter is an invitation into the life of faith as a process.

Listening to Paul/Listening to the Corinthians

First Corinthians reports one side of a very vigorous exchange between Paul and some parts of the Corinthian church. Paul argues powerfully for what he thought was right, and sometimes his language waxes hot: "Am I to come to you with a stick, or with love in a spirit of gentleness?" (4:21b). At other times he is more relaxed and writes quietly and persuasively about the subject in hand: "Pursue love and strive for the spiritual gifts, and especially that you may prophesy" (14:1). Most readers of 1 Corinthians have almost automatically "sided" with Paul and have thought that those who disagreed with him were in the wrong. Scholarly books about this letter speak of Paul's "opponents" as if the two sides were squared off in an outright opposition, and we even read about the Corinthian "heretics" or "enthusiasts." One fine recent book speaks of "Paul's problem children," picking up on Paul's own reference to the Corinthians as his children in 4:14 (Charles Talbert, *Reading Corinthians*, 36, et al).* Are these negative terms justified?

It is time to make a fresh start on this question. The idea that Paul was always right comes from a theology of inspiration that assumes that inspiration works within the individual writer of Scripture. Most thoughtful writers on the inspiration of the Bible now think of inspiration as arising in the interaction of people in community, instead of being isolated in a single

---

*Works cited in the text are given by author and title only. For a full description, see the list of Works Cited at the end of the book.

writer. But this more social image of inspiration has just begun to make an impact on how we view the interchange between Paul and the church in Corinth.

If the Spirit was active as Paul and the Corinthians interacted and learned from one another, we should not assume that Paul's side of the discussion is the only part worth listening to. We ourselves may learn from both sides of the discussion. A further possibility is that in many cases at least, Paul was not "opposing" the Corinthians but mediating conflicts among them.

The interpretation of 1 Corinthians in this book will concentrate on the letter itself and thus on what Paul says. There is a very good reason for this: we have Paul's words before us. It is not easy to know the beliefs and actions of those people to whom he was writing; indeed, Paul himself may have misunderstood them at times. Also, this letter is a strong and wonderful statement in its own right. It is worth trying to appreciate it for what it is.

But at the same time, at critical points we shall have to consider Paul's dialogue partners as well, and take what they said as seriously as we can. There is more guesswork in discovering what Paul was dialoguing with than we would like. But some important outlines are clear, both on such a question as how the Spirit is present and on the question of the appropriate roles for women and men in the congregation, as well as others.

We note in passing that the whole question of what the issues were that Paul was addressing is made more complicated by the way 2 Corinthians seems to be dealing with a different set of issues. By the time that letter (or collection of parts of letters) was written, new questions had arisen.

The City and the Church

Next, a word about the setting. The city of Corinth is one of the strategic centers of communication and commerce in its area. It is built on the isthmus of Corinth, controlling both an important overland route as well as the seagoing route that approaches it from the east and west. Nowadays this latter route is open to through traffic by the Corinth canal, but in Paul's day this freight had to be hauled over the isthmus. The location of Corinth makes it typical of the cities in which Paul chose to do most of his work in what is now Turkey and Greece. He usually worked in important centers of communication, and one can scarcely doubt that Paul foresaw the way in which the gospel message that he brought would spread out from these centers into neighboring areas.

The ancient city of Corinth had been destroyed by the Romans in 146 B.C.E., in the course of the Roman conquest of Greece. The city had been rebuilt by Julius Caesar about a century later, so that the city that Paul visited was not a place of ancient tradition but a city about a century old. The old city of Corinth had gained a name for luxury and undisciplined behavior. Whether or not that reputation was deserved, it had nothing to do with the Roman Corinth of Paul, though Paul's Corinth evidently also had its share of disorder—as any bustling, rough, commercial city does.

It was from a population of apparently very mixed background, but according to Paul mostly from the disadvantaged classes, that the Christian community was gathered (1:26–29). There were both slaves and free persons in the congregation, as well as both Jews and non-Jews (7:17–24). As far as we can tell from this letter and from 2 Corinthians, the question of how Jews and non-Jews were to belong together in the church was not a problem in Corinth as it was in some of Paul's other churches.

To judge in more detail about what sort of people were members of the congregation, we have to rely for the most part on indirect evidence. An important study makes the point that many of those who were drawn into the new faith in Corinth were uprooted from a fixed social location. That is, they had broken out of their traditional status and were seeking a more satisfying one—which was not easy to do in the socially rigid ancient world. Such people may have been socially "unimportant" in some regards, but were finding a place for themselves in others. The shifting social status of many of the new members would help us to understand the impatience of some of them with established ways and moral standards. (See Wayne A. Meeks, *The First Urban Christians*. This book is informative about the Corinthian correspondence in many ways.)

The Occasion for 1 Corinthians

Paul wrote 1 Corinthians from Ephesus, across the Aegean Sea (16:8). The letter tells us that he had founded the church in Corinth (3:10), and it presupposes a fairly lengthy stay in Corinth by Paul, as well as a period of absence long enough for him to have already written them one letter (5:9). By correlating these data with the narrative of the book of Acts, and with our knowledge of ancient history, 1 Corinthians can be dated close to 54 C.E. Acts 18:12 mentions that Paul was brought into court before Gallio, the proconsul of Achaia, which was the province of which Corinth was the capital. Gallio, the younger brother of the philosopher and public figure Seneca, was proconsul, probably for a term of one year that began in the spring of either 51 or 52, as we know from a famous inscription bearing his name which was found at Delphi. Paul's departure and subsequent travels as sketched in Acts 18—19 would fill the time to about 54 C. E. The date, of course, can be only approximate, particularly since thoughtful students have different opinions about the relation between the primary source for Paul, his own letters, and the principal secondary source, the book of Acts.

As for the later history of 1 Corinthians, it is quoted by 1 Clement, and also actually mentioned by him (1 Clem. 47:1–3), and it is also quoted by Ignatius of Antioch (Ign. *Eph.* 16:1; 18:1; *Trall.* 12:3; *Romans.* 4:3, etc.). Clement wrote in Rome about 95, Ignatius in Asia Minor about 112. This testimony to the existence and honored place of 1 Corinthians is as strong and as early as for any book of the New Testament.

Coming specifically to the occasion for the letter, in Ephesus Paul had received news from Corinth, news that provoked the letter. He mentions three sources of news. (1) Chloe's people (1:11) brought an oral report. It is not clear whether Chloe's "people" (servants? slaves?) were from Corinth or whether they were from the church in Ephesus where Paul then was, and had returned after a visit to Corinth. We usually suppose that they were Corinthians. (2) A letter came from the Corinthians (7:1). Probably many, perhaps most, of the questions dealt with after 7:1 were raised by this letter. (3) News arrived through Stephanas, Fortunatus, and Achaicus (16:17). They seem to have come as representatives of the church in Corinth, and they may have brought the letter from Corinth, though Paul does not say so. The combination of written and oral news showed Paul that there were strong differences between what he thought was right and what some people in Corinth believed and practiced, and to these differences, as he

5

understood them, he made the vigorous response that we now read in 1 Corinthians.

Paul was also getting in touch with Corinth through his representative, Timothy, whom he had already sent (4:17), but who had not yet arrived (16:10). Perhaps Timothy was en route around the Aegean Sea to the north, via Macedonia, as Paul himself planned to go (16:5).

We know little about how the letter was received. As we noted above, it is surprising that 2 Corinthians, which also reflects strong tensions between Paul and the church, deals with a new set of problems. We do not know how the questions to which 1 Corinthians responds were settled. It is clear that the question of Paul's authority continued to be a thorny one. For 2 Corinthians refers to an unsuccessful, painful visit by Paul to Corinth (2 Corinthians 2:1), as well as to a stern letter of reproof (2 Corinthians 2:4; 7:8), which cannot be our 1 Corinthians, since it has a different tone. Parts of the stern letter, however, may be incorporated into the present letter that we know as 2 Corinthians. It appears that after all these letters and visits, there was finally a reconciliation between Paul and the church in Corinth (2 Corinthians 1:1–11). Nevertheless, it is sobering to read that later in the century the church at Corinth was once again full of faction and bitterness (1 Clement 44; 46; 47).

The Form of 1 Corinthians

So far we have presupposed that 1 Corinthians as we have it now is one unified letter. Its status as genuinely from Paul can scarcely be doubted, and has not been seriously challenged. Yet whether 1 Corinthians was written all at once as a single, unified letter is very much an open question. In that sense its history is obscure. It may be a "letter" that was put together by a later editor from portions of two or more letters that Paul had written on separate occasions. Before trying to decide about the letter's unity, we will look first at the form of the letter. This will help us deal with the historical question of whether Paul wrote it all at once. Also it will help us to think about our hearing or reading of it as an ancient letter.

Of the many letters in the New Testament, none is more shaped by being a letter than 1 Corinthians. How does that affect the modern reader?

First, the letter form makes crystal clear to us that we are not the original audience for the letter. A reader can enter into some of the other New Testament literary forms—a gospel narrative or a hymn, for instance—without thinking about the difference between the original audience and the modern reader. But 1 Corinthians is shaped so fully by Paul's effort to communicate with *his* particular audience that it speaks to us more indirectly. We cannot simply identify with the Corinthians. This is evident from the fact that modern readers tend to identify with Paul rather than with the Corinthians who received the letter (we would identify with them if we read the letter as sent to *us*), a point to which we shall return.

Nevertheless, the letter form will be an essential ingredient in our reading of 1 Corinthians. Most obviously, as we read, we are constantly aware that we are hearing only half the conversation, so to speak. Though Paul's statements have often been read as finished and timeless dogmas, it is hard to read 1 Corinthians without being aware of the unfinished, open, occasional, "letter" quality of 1 Corinthians. The letter was shaped by what his audience had written to him and what Paul had learned about them, as well as by the past history of his dealings with them. It was intended to provoke a response that we only imperfectly know. First Corinthians itself indicates that it had a place in a continuing dialogue, in which Paul had been accused of changing his mind, or at least of not saying clearly what he meant (5:9–13), and in the course of which he almost certainly did express different sides of the questions that came up. The series of visits and letters of Paul to Corinth beautifully illustrate the communication of the gospel as a process, a dialogue calling for clarification on both sides. What Paul had to say could not simply be said once and for all.

There was an authoritarian side to Paul, and it appears in 1 Corinthians. But this letter, seen in the context of a dialogue between Paul and the Corinthians, shows an aspect of his message that has too often been overlooked. Many times he did not answer the questions that were laid before him, but put the decision in the hands of the hearers. Should I eat meat that had been sacrificed to pagan gods (chapters 8 and 10)? Should I get married (chapter 7)? Should I speak in tongues (chapter 14)? To these and other urgent questions Paul in substance says, "I am not telling you 'yes' or 'no.' You have to decide for yourself. Here are some elements and some limits to take into account in

7

making the decision." Such an approach could also be expressed in an essay or a treatise. But the letter form makes Paul's emphasis on responsible freedom dramatically clear. Christian teachers and preachers will do well to ponder Paul's practice, because it is such a temptation to tell people what the answer is when they ask.

It was a commonplace in Paul's time to speak of a letter as half a conversation and even as "a picture of…[the writer's] own soul" (Demetrius On Style, §227, quoted by William G. Doty, *Letters in Primitive Christianity*, 9). Yet in spite of what we would expect from this description, most of the personal letters of the time tended to be rather factual and unemotional. Ancient readers understood such letters as the accepted substitute for personal presence. Knowing that ancient letters usually were quite formal helps us to appreciate better the passionate intensity of 1 Corinthians, which is anything but formal. It must have been a great surprise when it arrived.

The intensity of this letter, which gives it, even centuries later, a remarkable freshness, does not mean that it is without structure. Paul followed a general pattern in writing his letters, and 1 Corinthians follows this pattern, though not in a fully typical way. An opening greeting and words of closing are almost inevitable in a letter of any size; Paul regularly expanded the greeting with a thanksgiving as he did here. The greeting and thanksgiving put him in touch with his audience and point to the direction in which the letter will move. The conclusion deals mostly with practical details including, often, Paul's travel plans. In between comes the main substance or body of the letter. In most of Paul's epistles the body is a basic statement of faith. In some cases this central section or "body" of the letter is followed by a section of exhortation or *paranesis*. There is no such clearly marked division in 1 Corinthians between basic statement of faith and exhortation, which is one of the stronger arguments against its unity. The letter moves back and forth between basic statements of faith, reflection about the church in Corinth and its life, and bits of exhortation, in a way that frustrates its alignment into the formal letter outline that we expect.

The Outline and Unity of 1 Corinthians

The plan of 1 Corinthians can be sketched as follows:

Introduction 1:1–9
  Greeting 1:1–3
  Thanksgiving 1:4–9
Body of the Letter 1:10—4:21
Aspects of the Transformation by Faith
  Divisions in the Church 1:10–17
  From Practical Behavior to Basic Faith 1:18–31
  Wisdom and Foolishness 2:1–16
  All Is God's Gift 3:1–23
  The Challenge to Paul's Authority 4:1–21
Specific Issues: Aspects of Community 5:1—15:58
  Questions of Personal Behavior in Community 5:1—11:1
    A Community Defiled by Violation of a Taboo 5:1–13
    A Community Divided by Litigation 6:1–11
    The Body Belongs to Christ 6:12–20
    Marriage and Relations Between Men and Women 7:1–40
    Love and Knowledge in Conflict Over Food Sacrificed to Idols 8:1—11:1
    Love and Knowledge 8:1–13
    Paul as an Example 9:1–27
    The Threat of Idolatry: An Example from the Past 10:1–13
    Participation in the Lord's Supper 10:14–22
    Freedom and Consideration Again 10:23—11:1
  Behavior at Worship 11:2—14:40
    Decorum in Worship 11:2–16
    True Sharing in the Lord's Supper 11:17–34
    Diversity of Gifts and One Spirit 12:1–31a
    Love as the Highest Gift 12:31b—13:13
    Being Carried Beyond Oneself versus Understanding and Sharing 14:1–40
  The Fulfillment of the Community in the Resurrection 15:1–58
Closing Words 16:1–24

The merit of seeing the letter on this plan is that it separates the cohesive section, 1:10—4:21, as the major "body" of the letter, from what follows, which is more diverse in subject. Further, 4:19–21 deals with Paul's travel plans, which often come at the very end of a letter, a sign at any rate that a section is ending, and an argument to some that the letter that began at 1:1 originally ended at 4:21. The rest as we now have it was added from other Pauline materials, according to this view.

A strong case can be made for such an analysis. (See Robert W. Funk, *Language, Hermeneutic, and Word of God*, 263–274, esp. 272. For other partition theories, see the major commentaries.)

I do not, however, see the need to appeal to a theory of composition from originally separate letters to understand the structure of 1 Corinthians. Here Paul did follow the normal way of framing his message with greeting, thanksgiving, and conclusion. But the striking thing about the main central section, including both "body" (1:10—4:21) and "specific issues," (5:1—15:58) is that it does not really permit a separation between basic affirmation of faith and exhortation or practical application to life. The two elements are intimately interwoven from start to finish. Though we have termed the "body" a basic statement of faith, it actually begins with a thoroughly "practical" exhortation about factions in the church, which leads eventually to a discussion of the transformation of life brought about by faith. Then the following section, chapters 5 through 15, is taken up with a series of issues raised by the behavior and questions of the Corinthians. It is a long section, and one that closes, rather than opening, with a basic statement of faith, the great chapter on the resurrection.

Thus the coherence of the letter as we have it is a good reason to take it as one unified composition.

Faith and Its Ethical Application

In this letter Paul departed from a frequent pattern that moved from "basic statement" to "application." The directness with which he tried to face the concrete situation at Corinth seems to have broken down the pattern that he sometimes followed in writing his letters. The loss of this conventional pattern is the more understandable when we see that in many smaller sections of the letter this distinction also breaks down, so that "basic faith" is approached from the side of application as much as the other way about. We come to see that what looked like a theoretical question about the form of the letter has brought us to the heart of the message, for modern readers as well as for ancient ones.

In a more reflective mood, it works well to set forth the basic meaning of faith first, and then proceed to application—as Paul so powerfully did in Romans, which he wrote from Corinth probably not long after he wrote 1 Corinthians. Christian thinkers have almost always said that the more organized statement of Romans is the place to begin, if one is to understand Paul's gospel. They have bypassed 1 Corinthians precisely because it deals so constantly with application, with Christian behavior. But this pervasive judgment arises from what can only be called a prejudice in favor of the way of speaking of faith that is possible when we stand at a distance from it and reflect about it. Perhaps the greatest challenge of 1 Corinthians to the modern reader is the challenge to rediscover the way in which faith and action arise from each other and interpenetrate each other.

In many ways one can come more directly to the heart of Paul's message from 1 Corinthians than from any other of his letters. It offers the fullest presentation of "faith in action," of the interpenetration of faith and action, responding as it does to a wide range of urgent questions, many of them arising from what Paul believed was an incomplete hearing of the gospel. The letter offers an important reminder that many people do not "begin" with faith but begin where they are with their baffling questions of behavior in which faith manifests itself more or less adequately. To follow the lead of 1 Corinthians would be to go directly to questions of behavior and from these to try to clarify how faith is involved. When one approaches faith this way, the distinction between "basic statement of faith" and "application" fades away. This is so in 1 Corinthians not just because of the pressure of urgent questions that Paul had to try to answer, though that pressure probably did lead to his loosening the traditional rhetoric of letter writing. But he was able to do this because the inner dynamic of his subject matter was congenial to it. When he came to grapple with their problems, he did not have to lay out a basic statement of faith first, because faith could equally well be spoken of in terms of Christian behavior.

Radical Transformation and Continuing Responsibility

The issues that brought tension to the church at Corinth will be dealt with in detail in the commentary. But all of the

specific problems are held together by the central theme that
faith works a radical transformation in life, a transformation
that makes a change in how one actually behaves. Paul and the
Corinthians agreed on this point, but Paul wrote the letter because he believed that many of them badly misunderstood what
the behavior was that flowed from faith, and thus must have
misunderstood faith itself. Some of them seem to have thought
that he did not carry the transformation of faith far enough.

Christ brings a new power and direction into life, so fundamental that old values and attachments are not important, and
yet many of these old values nonetheless are taken up into the
new life. We can say that they are met again in the new life—
transformed or revised, or perhaps simply reinforced. The new
power of Christ and of the Spirit is from beyond ourselves, and
puts us in touch with a reality beyond the world we have previously known. This is a real transformation. We are not the same,
and we can be free from the values and standards that are preva-
lent in the "world"—in the average society around us. All the
partners to the discussion agreed to such a point of view.

But in addition, some, at least, of the Corinthians seem to
have believed that the transformation of their lives through
Christ detached them so thoroughly from their preceding existence that when they returned to it, they could be free from
many of the world's conventions. The roles of men and women,
some kinds of sexual behavior, traditions of clothing style, relations with people of different religious practice—these were
some of the questions where some of them seem to have believed that Paul was not ready to go far enough in changing the
traditional patterns.

We often approach this question in terms of our "freedom."
The question of freedom does appear in 1 Corinthians (6:12; 9:1),
though not frequently. Without usually casting his thought in
these terms, Paul nevertheless insisted that freedom leads us
back into the world of responsibility for fellow human beings.
As we shall see, he was sometimes too ready to view responsibility in terms of established social conventions. Yet no freedom can be exercised without consideration of the setting within
which one lives. Merely to speak of freedom is to think about
one's life too individualistically, which may be why Paul does
not often use this term. Life as interaction was closer to his vision of true humanity. There was room for great variety in the
interaction, the open community, which he believed the church

to be—though he was also hampered by unexamined presuppositions about what behavior was socially acceptable in community. Some of the Corinthians, it seems, wanted the church to be open to even more variety. Neither then nor now can this be an easy question to resolve.

Self-consciousness and Love

There is no doubt that, through the centuries, Christian faith was one of the principal forces that aroused the individual's self-consciousness in Western culture, and made Western people think about their freedom and their separate existence. Paul was at the center of this process. His message put a strong emphasis on faith as freedom from one's past—set forth here in terms of the cross and elsewhere, especially in Romans, in terms of "justification by faith"—as against confidence in one's own achievements. These emphases surely stimulated a far greater inwardness and a reflection about one's inner spiritual state than had been common before his time. The language of justification does occur in 1 Corinthians (1:30; 4:4; 6:11; that these are all the Greek words usually translated "justify" or "justification" does not show very clearly in the NRSV), but the image of justification is not central here as it is in Romans and Galatians. The direct preoccupation with one's state before God, of course, did not begin with Paul, but it finds a powerful expression in his writings. And from Paul flowed an impetus to reflect on one's inner state, seen later on in classic form in Augustine's Confessions. This impetus has continued into our modern self-questioning and introspection, both in the circle of faith and more broadly in modern culture. In this sense Paul could be said to be one of the great originating impulses for the modern interest in psychology. We rightly associate him with the discovery of the immense weight of the solitary self's destiny that has been a mark of Christian history and that has in modern times diffused broadly in Western culture.

Thus the note of reflection about one's inmost self, its guilt and forgiveness, its potentialities, and its future, has important anchorage in Paul. Such self-examination is in a sense our fate as inheritors of the Pauline tradition. Yet we fail to hear what Paul is saying, and in particular we fail to hear what Paul is saying in 1 Corinthians, if we put the emphasis on that side of his message. For in this letter, in response to the various prob-

13

lems of the church, Paul was repeatedly trying to bring them back again, out of their preoccupation with their inner selves, into the interpersonal world of human interaction. Whether he is dealing with factions in the church (chapters 1, 3, 4), with wisdom (chapter 2), with aberrations in the field of sexual behavior (chapters 5 and 6), with the Lord's Supper (chapter 11), or with the broader question of different functions in the church (chapters 12, 14), Paul consistently urges his hearers that faith does not simply release them from connection with other human beings into a private world with God, but calls them back in love (chapter 13) to release the energies of their selves in true human interaction. Also the chapter on the resurrection (chapter 15) concludes: "in the Lord your labor is not in vain" (15:58c), where he is thinking of *labor* in its interpersonal aspect of what we do for one another, what we do to create an open community, which is thus done for the Lord.

The consistent theme of Paul's letter, calling for what can be called "separation *and* return," was a response to a direction of faith development in the church that we understand only very imperfectly in its details. In modern scholarly study it is commonly called a beginning form of gnosticism or a state of inward faith moving in the direction of gnosticism. (See the discussion below on chapters 1—4.) We may perhaps best see a comparison in the "New Age" movements of our own time, since both what Paul addresses and the "New Age" movements emphasize a break with tradition, an intense inner life of faith, often in the form of ecstatic experience, and a sharp separation between soul and body. Very different, but also helpful for a thoughtful comparison, are the Pentecostal churches with their emphasis not only on speaking with tongues (as in 1 Corinthians 14) but on intense, extraordinary religious experience as a mark of the Spirit's presence. Whatever the details were, and there were apparently several different styles of faith in the church, the Corinthian Christians strongly emphasized their inner experience and the radical transformation worked by the presence of Christ's Spirit and by faith. They found this new realm of experience so engrossing that they believed that all, or at least many, of the crucial forms of social relationship were either changed or no longer important. At least that is how it appeared to Paul. Through the centuries interpreters of the New Testament have usually been very negative toward that inner, dualistic type of faith known as gnosticism. Today it is time for a fresh look, just as it is with the "New Age" movements and the Pentecostal churches. One-sided as they were and are, it is important to try to understand them and what they have to teach.

It is important to remember that Paul, too, put heavy weight on the inner side of faith, though without the introspection that we engage in. Very likely the "proto-gnostics," if that is the right way to think of them, and the ecstatics in the church had learned from Paul himself much of the direction that they took. He, like them, believed that Christ brought about a radical transformation that cut people off from their old forms of life, even from their old selves. But for him, this movement of separation was followed by a return, in which the old relationships and responsiblities were again confronted, now in a new way. Some of them believed that he saw this return to interpersonal responsibilities in too traditional a way. It will be an important part of the study of 1 Corinthians to see this dialogue at work, a dialogue between an understanding of faith as separation on the part of the people he was writing to, and a richer view of faith as separation and return on the part of Paul.

Since the tendency to turn religious experience into a private affair is one of the principal features of the life of the church today, as well as of religious life in general in our time, Paul's reflections about how faith both releases the believers from the world and then draws them back into human responsibility in a new way can be a key guide to the relevance of the letter today.

Then and Now: Different Problems and a Common Quest

There is a real obstacle to our reading 1 Corinthians in this way. It is this: the concrete problems that appear in the letter are either very different from our own (for instance, food offered to pagan gods) or, though the problem is the same, it is set in a different a context and history, so that we cannot directly apply Paul's solutions to our own situation (for instance, marriage and the relations between men and women). We shall miss the value and meaning of 1 Corinthians if we read it only to find out the "answers" to the problems at stake. In the first place, as noted above, Paul often does not provide an answer. And more than that, even on some points about which he believes very strongly that his insight or answer must be the only correct one, we must be ready to inquire whether it is some cultural history that we no longer share that has provided Paul with his point of view, or whether he is expressing some deeper ethical insight that may be taken directly into our journey of faith.

It is clear that few today hold to the unchanging validity of this letter's command that women must always have their heads veiled in church (11:2–16; this passage is, however, more obscure than the common translation suggests). As will become clear in the analysis of chapter 7, similar questions must be asked about many of the stands that Paul takes about the relations between men and women.

Even more than this, the point can be made that it is possible and appropriate for a Christian of our time to take part in a religious ceremony of another faith in a way that would have been quite impossible for Paul, for whom that would have been sheer idolatry (10:14). Rather than feel uncomfortable about this situation, the reader would be wise to acknowledge it in full and rejoice in the freedom that it implies and demands.

Some readers will wish that Paul had had the opportunity to reflect, to gain more perspective on the issues which he discussed. Then, they may say, he would have been able to write a more systematic and fundamental statement of the faith that lay behind his responses to the specific issues. But we may be grateful that it did not work out that way. Though the modern reader may be distant from many of the problems of 1 Corinthians, he or she can, in reading this letter, more fully enter into the interchange between the struggle with a difficult issue and the reach toward the basic faith that lies behind it, than we would be likely to do with a letter that had worked out a more systematic statement of the underlying faith in relative independence from specific problems. Thus the process of seeking for a way to relate faith to life—a process that by its nature is always unfinished and open—is what one discovers so profoundly in 1 Corinthians.

It is perhaps only natural that as we read 1 Corinthians our first reaction is to identify with Paul and to join in his criticisms of the imperfect Corinthians. In the "story" of Paul's dealings with the church, we have usually thought of ourselves as on Paul's side. But we must also try to enter into the other side of the dialogue. As we learn to do this, we shall be better able to appreciate both how recurrent are the tendencies that the Corinthians expressed, and how these tendencies represent real and deep spiritual concerns, as well as how difficult it is to live in the way Paul urged them.

The difference between Paul and some parts of the congregation was described above in terms of radical transformation, and the question of how radical transformation is to be related to the ongoing responsibilities of life. Another way of putting it is to ask, "What is a truly open community, in which variety is prized while mutual respect springs from a shared vision?" To focus on this question will help us see what Paul was trying to bring about. An open community calls for a precarious balance between the welcoming of a variety of people on the one hand, and the self-discipline of searching for and renewing a common vision on the other. The tension between these two aspects of an open community is an important clue to the dynamic of 1 Corinthians.

With these general considerations in mind, we now turn to 1 Corinthians itself.

1:1–9 INTRODUCTION:

Greeting and Thanksgiving

The Introduction skillfully lays out the groundwork for the important controversial points that will follow. In a conventional letter, the introduction would be very brief, including only the name of the sender and the recipient(s), and a wish for their health. Sometimes this greeting would be followed by a word of thanks to God. As was his custom, Paul expanded this short conventional form to make the opening serve as a real introduction to what follows.

Here the greeting (verses 1–3) includes a definition of Paul's authority and a word about the true status of those who receive the letter. There are some uncertainties about the exact wording of the Greek and about the way in which the different phrases are related to each other, but these do not affect the basic thrust of the greeting. All, both Paul and the Corinthians, are bound together as those who have received the gift and call of Christ. This point is made by the paralleling of "Paul, called to be an apostle" with "the church...called to be saints."

In 1 Corinthians Paul speaks often of the "church" (*ekklesia*). He uses the word both for the local congregation and for the whole community of believers. Perhaps this is the point of the way in which the greeting is extended to all believers "in every place" (verse 2), which is rather surprising since the letter itself is specifically directed to the situation at Corinth.

"Sanctified in Christ Jesus" and "saints" both mean those who are set apart as belonging to God. Taken together with the word "called," the greeting is a strong reminder that the church

19

and its members do not stand on their own resources and achievements, but on the call that comes from God. How important it was to remind them of this, the rest of the letter will show.

Paul too is "called," and does not stand on his own resources. He will emphasize later how unconventional his authority is (4:8–13) and how he does not deserve it (15:8–11). Nevertheless, the greeting from an apostle, standard in almost all of his letters, reminds the Corinthians that Paul is a representative of Christ and that as such he claims some kind of authority. Paul's companion Sosthenes is also included in the greeting, but we note that he is not called an apostle but simply a "brother," a fellow Christian; he does not share Paul's authority. Since many of the members of the church at Corinth were reluctant to accept Paul's authority simply on his say-so, we shall have to reflect later about his authority. (See "Paul as Apostle," pp. 42–45.)

The conventional wish that the correspondent may be well is here transformed (not by Paul alone, but by a line of tradition in which he stands) into a kind of blessing. "Peace" is now coming again to be a conventional greeting, with us at the end of a letter along with the sender's name. It was then also conventional especially in Jewish tradition. Paul adds one of his favorite terms for God's gift, "grace." The wish for well-being, like the naming of the recipients as saints just before, serves as a reminder of the constant giving of God through Christ, a giving that sets the ambience within which they live.

The final element in the Introduction, again a customary one, is a word of thanksgiving. Paul transforms it into a prayer of thanksgiving that highlights what he and they can agree on. Throughout the paragraph, there is repeated emphasis on the way in which the life and experience of faith are sheer gift. Later it will appear that Paul thinks that some of them tend to forget this.

The importance of "speech" and "knowledge," as well as of "spiritual gifts," in Corinth will soon be apparent in the rest of the letter. It is often noticed how tactfully Paul begins by thanking God for what he shares with them, before coming to the controversial points, and that is surely how he approaches his correspondents. He appeals to their common ground with him. It would be wrong to regard these words of appreciation as mere rhetoric. Despite their sharp differences, Paul deeply believed that they shared the same life in community.

Closer reading shows also that the thanksgiving, though it does not mention the threats that Paul believed existed in Corinth, subtly prepares the way for discussing them by its emphasis that God's work is not yet complete. The "revealing of our Lord Jesus Christ" (verse 7) is still to come. Chapter 15, on the resurrection, will return to this point in the climax of the letter. Later Christians came to speak very naturally of the revelation that had already taken place with the coming of Christ. Here Paul speaks of the revelation or revealing (the Greek word for the two is the same) as something that the believer is still waiting for. This way of putting it is in harmony with the strong emphasis later in the letter on the paradoxical tension—the incompleteness—in the continuing present-day existence of the believer, and on the cross as the way in which Christ is present. To put it strongly, though Paul does not speak of the precariousness of the believer's state, the very mention that Christ will "strengthen you to the end" (verse 8) is a reminder that even the life of faith is a life of struggle.

1:10—4:21 THE "BODY" OF THE LETTER:

Divisions in the Church and Wisdom Misunderstood

The first main section of 1 Corinthians (1:10—4:21), which is the "body" or principal thesis of the letter, combines an urgent practical concern, the problem of divisions in the church, with a statement of the fundamental basis on which faith rests. Paul says that the divisions have come about because of a failure to grasp the fundamental basis of faith.

The intimate interaction between faith and life is thus a mark of 1 Corinthians from the start, and there is no better place in the New Testament to confront and learn about this interaction. That it is a complex one is shown by the form in which Paul sets forth his discussion. He did not move systematically from one topic to the next, but enriched the readers' insight by moving back and forth between the practical behavioral questions and the fundamentals of faith. The general plan of the section can be abbreviated as A B A'. That is, the practical question of divisions in the church comes up first (A: 1:10–17); then comes the presentation of the basis for faith (B: 1:18—2:16); and then the letter returns to the practical questions in the light of the fundamentals just discussed (A': 3:1—4:21). This pattern of A B A' is a frequent one in 1 Corinthians, and if we notice it, we can more easily understand the flow of Paul's writing. It was a common pattern of rhetorical presentation in the Hellenistic world, in contrast to the more usual straight line of the development of thought usually found in essays and sermons today. Recognizing it will help a reader to see how Paul achieved the powerful effects that he did in his writing, and will show that what often seems on first reading to be an unplanned and shifting focus of attention first on one theme and then on another is usually thoughtfully designed. At the same time, there are also abrupt and spontaneous changes in the direction of Paul's thought at times.

Even these brief remarks about the plan of these chapters are a reminder that Paul was a skilled and careful writer. Otherwise, he would not have produced such letters as he did. Thus, one needs to see his remarks about his lack of human skills of communication (1:17; 2:1) in the light of his actually very skillful and effective practice. Paul was by no means as "anti-cultural" as he sounds at times. He did strongly believe that cultural achievement could not possibly give a foundation for life; such a foundation came only from faith. Yet he was deeply saturated in writing skills, though not in a formal, school-taught way (and, we may safely assume, in speaking skills as well, if not conventional ones, in spite of the taunt of his opponents which he cites in 2 Corinthians 10:10). One could say that in spite of his rejection of the "wisdom of this age" (2:6), he made ample use of it. The very form of his letters thus introduces the reader to the heart of a basic theological problem, and warns against too hasty a reading of Paul's rejection of wisdom. We shall have to return to this issue.

The plan of these chapters is complicated by two elements that intrude upon the simple A B A' pattern. For one thing, the presentation of the basis of faith is a complex one, which both contrasts the cross of Christ with human wisdom, and then surprisingly endorses wisdom of the right kind. But more important still for the organization of this part of the letter, an entirely different factor is imposed upon the basic pattern: Paul's own role in Corinth. The section is almost as much about Paul's vocation as apostle as it is about the Corinthians and their divisions and their claim to wisdom. No aspect of these chapters is worth closer attention than the way in which the "I" of Paul keeps appearing with more and more insistence as he proceeds. Few contemporary witnesses to the Christian faith would dare to intrude their personal vocation as directly into their message as Paul did—or if they did, we would be offended at their pride. Yet Paul brings in his personal vocation precisely as a testimony to faith in the cross with its rebuke of pride, while at the same time showing an immense confidence in the rightness and authority of his claims. The complex interweaving of Paul's assertions that he is "[not]...anything" (3:7) with his repeated demands for the recognition of his own authority (especially in 4:14–21) is as illuminating for our understanding of Christian existence as the things that he says directly about the Corinthians. This again is a theme that will require further study.

We shall survey the thought of this whole passage in its main sections, and then reflect on these main topics that dominate it: the Spirit, wisdom, the cross, and Paul's vocation as apostle.

1:10–17 Divisions in the Church

The first main section turns directly to the report from Chloe's people that there are divisions in the church. There is no indication that the divisions had led to separate groups for worship; in that sense the congregation was still united. (But we have to remember that we do not really know how large the church in Corinth was, or how the meetings of smaller groups were coordinated with the times when they all came together.) But there evidently were great strains upon the unity of the church. The divisions showed up in the fact that different groups appealed to different "founding individuals" on whom they looked as establishing and defining their faith (and, presumably, their lifestyle as well): Paul, Apollos, Cephas (Peter), and Christ. We know from what immediately follows (1:13–17) that, sometimes, at least, part of this special attachment was derived from a relation to the person who had baptized the believer; Paul denied that a group could be built around him, since he had baptized so few. Oddly, he did not seem to remember just whom he had baptized; perhaps his indefiniteness was a way of putting down the importance of the question in the first place. Christ, of course, had not baptized anyone at Corinth, and it is a real question whether there was a group at Corinth who said "I belong to Christ," or whether this is a phrase that Paul introduced to show the absurdity of the whole proceeding. Another view is that the "Christ party" were the extreme spiritualists. To Paul, in any case, all of them belonged to Christ.

It is possible that Peter had visited Corinth and baptized some new Christians, but that is only a possibility. Later on (3:4; see 3:1–9; 4:6) Paul cited only himself and Apollos as alternative persons to whom one might "belong" (Peter or Cephas does reappear at 3:22). It may be that the main dissension at Corinth was centered around the two names of Paul and Apollos. There has been much speculation about Apollos, but we simply do not know what he stood for, and it is important to note that Paul did not attribute a wrong basis for faith in Corinth to Apollos' teaching. We note that Apollos is mentioned in Acts 18:24—19:1, and is there called "eloquent." But this is too slender a basis to claim to understand the special emphasis of his proclamation.

It was not because he wanted all believers to be alike that Paul opposed the formation of groups. Quite to the contrary, a main theme of 1 Corinthians is Paul's insistence that there will be great variety among believers. In this opening section he does not say what is wrong about the existence of the different groups. Later on in his discussion it becomes clear that he criticizes the groups because he sees them as expressions of a self-assertive claim to be better than the others who belonged to other groups (3:3–4). Such a claim contradicts the basis of faith because it obscures the primary reality, that God had made their existence in faith possible, prior to any action of their own (1:27–31; 4:7). To put it in different terms, he says that the groups will give them a false sense of security and close them off to the real openness of faith, which includes openness to various and very different kinds of people.

1:18–31 From Practical Behavior to Basic Faith

The movement from practical behavior to basic faith takes place through a reference to Paul's own vocation, since he had come into the discourse as one sent not to baptize but to preach. His preaching, of course, brought the basis for faith. This is one of the repeated places where Paul introduced his own position into the presentation of faith. Without clarifying further what he understood the different groups to stand for, he moved toward the deeper basis that should eliminate the tendency toward divisions altogether; he wrote, that is, against what he thought was common to all groups.

The controlling element in the first paragraph of this section (1:18–25) is the contrast between the cross of Christ and (human) wisdom; later a third term, the Spirit, also throws light on this contrast. This short paragraph is a key one for the whole letter.

1 CORINTHIANS

Much has been written about the beliefs of those in Corinth to whom Paul was writing, and one cannot try to interpret the letter without asking the question about what their beliefs were. After all, the letter form presupposes that the reader knows what the situation is. In a general way we can know what Paul was opposing, but it is both risky and unnecessary to develop too detailed a theory about the views that he opposed, as we noted above in the Introduction. We have only Paul's side of the conversation. On the one hand, he did not necessarily always understand what he was opposing or represent it accurately. On the other, what he writes has a large degree of coherence even without a statement from the other side. It will be important, however, to try to see how what Paul said was not satisfactory to some of the people at Corinth, especially to some of the women in the congregation.

"Wisdom" was one of the keys to Corinthian faith. Paul abruptly contrasted the wisdom of this age or this world with the cross of Christ. The question of power is prominent throughout the paragraph (1:18, [21], 24, 27). Wisdom evidently appealed because of its power, and against this Paul set the paradoxical power in weakness of the cross of Christ. Against human wisdom the cross looks like foolishness and weakness, but it is actually the focal place where God's surprising power to transform human existence is at work.

The wisdom that Paul combats, despite its appeal of offering power, was not the wisdom that gives the technological power that modern people associate with the maxim, "wisdom is power." The two kinds of wisdom are not unrelated, for modern technological wisdom includes a large component of power to control other people. The dimension of control was also a feature of ancient wisdom, which arose in part precisely in the effort to control existence. But for the people of Paul's time, wisdom did not move in the direction of the detailed and systematic empirical study that is the basis of modern technological efforts. Instead, it moved in precisely the opposite direction, toward penetrating the ultimate mysteries.

Thus, when Paul spoke of wisdom as "the wisdom of the world" (1:20) or as "human wisdom" (2:5), he was setting a limit to wisdom that presumably was not recognized by some of the Corinthians. The wisdom that Paul was opposing was prized because it was thought to give a special and privileged knowledge of God, and this was the source of the power that was found in it. Ecstatic revelation was the culmination of wisdom in Corinth, and, though Paul did not oppose experiences of ecstasy, he set the cross of Christ over against any claim that wisdom could give power by putting one in touch with the ultimate. The cross seemed like foolishness because it involved giving up the claim to "be someone" and it meant giving up the kind of power, Paul thought, that made the Corinthians so proud of their wisdom.

The same point is made "sociologically," in terms of the social composition of the Corinthian church, in the next paragraph (1:26–31). The group in Corinth, he says, did not contain many who were "wise by human standards" (literally, "according to the flesh"). The "not many" may be ironic and really mean "not any." It is far more probable, however, that there were some in the congregation with cultural and economic advantages. Such social differences, in fact, were probably part of the reason for the emergence of the conflicting groups that Paul had just been criticizing. But Paul makes the point that most of the congregation came from the disadvantaged, economically struggling classes, including, as we know from 7:21–24, both slaves and free persons. Some of the latter were, no doubt, recently freed slaves. (For more on the social condition of the church at Corinth, see Wayne A. Meeks, *The First Urban Christians*.)

There are those who interpret ecstatic religious experience as a compensation for social disadvantage. That is an oversimplification, but the background of 1 Corinthians as written to a group of little or no leverage and power in the everyday affairs of life cannot be left aside as one interprets it. Paul turns the barrenness of their economic and cultural life to the service of his point: even without any of these cultural advantages, God has worked through Christ to give them a new life. As the remarks about boasting and the final quotation from Jeremiah 9:24 make clear, the issue is the grounds on which one is to find a way of seeking approval or acceptance by God, which includes what we call accepting oneself. Authentic approval of oneself can rest only on a gift from God, and not on one's possession of status.

The statements of this paragraph speak of daily human reality from the perspective of the *cross* (though this word does not appear). What one sees in and receives from the cross is shown by the way in which what seems of no account is transformed by God, who is at work in the little community.

27

Further, this passage has extreme significance for the modern reader in a quite different way. In bringing to expression the situation of these early Christians, the section is a sharp reminder of how different the function of the church was in those days: it did not have the prestige in the society and culture that it has now (even though that status is growing weaker). Its members were not responsible for the government, the social customs, or the economic practices of the day. The Christians were outsiders. There are still outsider congregations today, particularly in places like Latin America. But even congregations drawn from the disadvantaged sectors of today's society feel themselves a part of that society in ways that were not the case in Paul's day. The message of the cross as preached to them will be very different in its details from the message that Paul preached. Here lies a prime challenge to the interpreter: truly to inherit the line from Paul, and also to speak prophetically (as Paul here cites a prophet) to congregations that are not outsiders.

2:1–16 Wisdom and Foolishness

With the next section, 2:1–16, we come to Paul's central statement on wisdom, the more striking because it is both negative (2:1–5) and positive (2:6–16). The power that Paul found at work in himself and his vocation did not derive from his human wisdom, he says. This power was that of the cross of Christ. The first four verses are a strong negative statement about the Christian message; it does not depend upon "wisdom." Once again we see the interplay between Paul's statement of faith and his consciousness of his own personal involvement—"When *I* came to you…" (verse 1). The issue of power emerges again when he contrasts the seeming lack of power in his personal presence ("I came to you in weakness…" [verse 3]) with "a demonstration of the Spirit and of power" (verse 4) in his message. The point is that human wisdom does not offer what it promises, the power to be in control of one's life.

Then the attention shifts abruptly to a positive statement, that a wisdom that does not give a basis for the message, but derives from it, is indeed available to the "mature" (or "perfect") since it is taught by the Spirit. By juxtaposing these two contrasting statements about wisdom, Paul was able to explain how he could both reject the "common" wisdom and yet maintain that there is another kind, which is available when one advances beyond the elementary stages of faith. As he understood it, they were not ready for the wisdom of the perfect or mature. Just what this wisdom was Paul did not say. He may well have thought of it very much as his Corinthian counterparts did, as a special knowledge of divine things, partly received in ecstatic experience and partly from thinking, or he may have seen it more as a deepening of the paradoxical wisdom of the cross. For him, these two were not contradictory. That it was a special divine gift, so distant from the world that even the (spiritual) powers that govern the world did not know it, marks the separation between the true access to God's way through the cross, and the ascent to divine knowledge by speculative or ecstatic wisdom. We should note that later, Paul does combine his faith in Christ with wisdom, for instance in chapters 11, 13, and 15, in which he draws on wisdom traditions. Also the link to commonsense wisdom is preserved by the fact that a test of wisdom is its effects on social behavior. A wisdom that does not establish community is no wisdom at all.

That true wisdom is far beyond human nature is made clear by stating that it is a gift of the Spirit. The Spirit is a presence with God and with the believer. Unlike the powers of the world, the Spirit does understand the mysteries of God, and communicates them to the believer. Though the Spirit comes into the picture here primarily in connection with wisdom, Spirit brings transformation as well as understanding. Christ is not mentioned until the last verse of the section, but the whole presentation assumes that it is through the cross of Christ that the Spirit is made available to the believer.

The chapter concludes with a brief contrast between two types of human beings: those transformed by the Spirit, and the unspiritual or those not transformed by the Spirit (2:14–16). The tension and contrast in Paul's teaching about wisdom and the Spirit is well brought out by the fact that here the message returns to Christ, whose "mind" the believer has (verse 16), while at the same time returning to the question of power: the spiritual person is "subject to no one else's scrutiny" (verse 15). That the "judging" is related to the contest for authority in Corinth is shown by the way in which the same theme reappears in 4:1–5.

3:1–23 Missing the Point:
What Paul, Apollos, and the Others Were About

With chapter 3 the focus turns from the basis of faith back to the concrete Corinthian situation. There is reference back to 1:10–17 in 3:1–4; now the disputatious arrogating of a human leader's name to one's group can be seen to be precisely the opposite of what some of the Corinthians supposed it to be. It is not a sign of exalted spiritual experience, but the reassertion in religious guise of the old "flesh" or "merely human" existence. Paul presupposed here, as he did in the more developed contrast between flesh and spirit in Romans 7:13—8:39, that flesh is more than a mere biological base for human life. It is, in its present distorted form, a pervasive and destructive force in human existence, showing up in the strife of the groups in Corinth. Against it he set the contrasting pervasive force of the Spirit, just discussed, which if genuinely present would thoroughly transform human existence away from the conflictual, competitive way of the "merely human" or "flesh."

Along with the contrast of flesh and spirit another theme appears in the section, the contrast between the child and the adult. The two contrasts do not quite overlap, since the child/adult opposition presupposes that there is some continuity between one stage and the other, while the flesh/spirit contrast is usually presented as an abrupt change. The question of growth in faith was not of much interest to Paul, though he does use growth language elsewhere, as in Romans 5:3–5. Such language was widespread in the popular moral teaching of the day. Paul's lack of interest in growth in faith sprang from his confidence that the power of the Spirit was so great that if one turned to it, one would not need to develop patterns of moral or spiritual discipline to further growth. Nevertheless, the Corinthian church confronted him with a situation in which the transformation of existence was (he thought) extremely imperfect and incomplete, and in response to it he used the image of the undeveloped child. This image opened the way for later Christians to connect Paul's teachings to a wider interest in spiritual growth.

From this brief introduction, the focus quickly moves to Paul himself again. With the two images of gardening (3:5–9) and construction (3:10–15), he presents his work and that of those who follow him in such a way as to do two things: (1) to shift the attention away from the human worker (Paul, Apollos) to God who gave the energy and hence "deserved the credit"; and (2) to keep a place for the primacy of his own apostolic contribution nevertheless, through his position as planter of the seed or builder of the foundation.

These images are set in a framework of expectation. The gardening or construction is in process, and in the end it will be tested. The passage breathes a wonderful sense of the way in which human work can have lasting significance precisely in being focused away from the human doer to the task and to the giver of the power to work.

The conclusion that the work and the doer have related but separate fates—one who does well will be rewarded at the judgment, and one who does poorly will be deprived of reward but will not be destroyed—shows Paul's deep faith that membership in the community brought an irreversible change in a person. Even weak and failing members will be included in the final vindication of the church (note the case of the flagrant transgressor in 5:5, which is similar if not wholly parallel). The point is relevant to the discussion here under way because it drives home Paul's conviction that one does not have to cling to one's achievement to be accepted.

To these comparisons dealing with the founder and builders of the church is added a third, which turns again to the members themselves: they are the temple within which the Spirit of God lives, and as such are under God's protection (3:16–17). The shift from a building constructed by humans to a building in which God's Spirit lives (both images derived from apocalyptic expectation, that is, from the hope for a radical transformation of existence at the end of the world) keeps the emphasis on the temple as the community rather than as the individual person as many modern readers take it: you are God's *temple*, not God's *temples*. The "you" is a plural "you," emphasizing that they are all together in this transformation.

The concluding paragraph of this chapter (3:18–23) ties the basic reflection of chapter 2 to the practical ones of chapter 3, by returning to the subject of power and boasting that has been a central thread in the whole discussion. "Human" wisdom claims to offer a way to manage life successfully, but it is self-defeating, and its inability really to manage life shows up in the competitiveness that sets one group or leader against another. "...you should become fools so that you may become wise" (verse 18b); that is, accept the reversal of values that puts true community above the striving for status. That is the heart of God's struggle with the world, as Paul saw it. But for him access to God's victory is strictly through the cross of Christ.

4:1–21 The Challenge to Paul's Authority

The final chapter of the body of the letter (4:1–21) again brings the focus squarely upon Paul himself and upon the challenge to his authority that was implied by the existence of the competing groups at Corinth. Paul defended himself in a way that beautifully brings out the contrast between power and weakness that he had previously set forth as the mark of Christian existence generally (1:18–25). First (4:1–5) he defined himself as a "steward" or trustee, that is, as one who does not have an independent standing but is responsible to someone else. But that does not mean that he is responsible to the Corinthians! Quite the opposite. He argued from his status as trustee that they were in no position to judge him, as apparently some of them were in the process of doing. On the contrary, he is wholly responsible to the one who gave him his charge, and immune from any human judgment, even his own. The metaphor of the trustee, with its implication of a final accounting, points forward to the final judgment that suspends preliminary judgments. Confidence that judgment is in God's hands is an important point for Paul (cf. Romans 12:19–20). It meant that one could avoid the condemnatory judgments that people so easily make, since these matters are ultimately in God's hand. Here he applied this principle to himself, though confidently expecting vindication.

The application of this point to the Corinthians themselves follows in the next statement (4:6–7). Neither Paul nor Apollos is a basis on which one could be "puffed up" (verse 6; the phrase, "Nothing beyond what is written" is difficult to understand and may even be an addition to the text). As Paul himself was purely the receiver of a trust in the previous statement, he reminds them here that they, too, are purely receivers. Boasting is excluded.

How difficult it is to exclude boasting is shown in the next section (4:8–21), a powerfully ironic comparison of the Corinthians in their seeming position of success and attainment with Paul's position as apostle, a position that brings him into a whole list of negative, seemingly destructive situations. The move of defending one's position by listing the hardships into which it had brought one was well known in the popular Stoic rhetoric of the day. Paul's ethic had much in common with that popular morality, in the practical stance toward behavior that both advocated. Both Paul and the popular morality of the Stoics called for strength and integrity in courageously facing difficulties. Paul differed in making his resistance to difficulty a response to a gift that he had received, rather than a sign of his inner strength as with the popular Stoicism.

But this is not the only point to notice in the section. Perhaps even more important is the way in which, in his campaign against boasting or being "puffed up," Paul himself boasts in his own way. The contrast between Paul and the Corinthians, often taken to be merely a thrust at an aberration in Christian behavior (and it certainly was that), probes deeply into a fundamental tension in the Christian vision: the apostle aims to give his congregation the same gift that he has received. But the asymmetry of the relationship of giving, its one-sidedness, means that they tend to perceive the gift for what it brings to them, and they miss the full freedom to be deprived of good things that Paul had discovered. In part this is a lack of full insight on their part—hence Paul's bitter irony, making fun of their seemingly easy position. But this very asymmetry or one-sidedness is built into all giving in the spirit of love, which tends to treat the loved one more gently than oneself, thus easily leading the recipient to the one-sided perception of what it is to receive a gift, which Paul here ironically attacks.

There is another irony in the asymmetry of giving, an irony that lies behind Paul's whole effort to claim authority. His aim was to help them find the freedom really to live together; they should be able to get along without him. Some of them believed that they could very well do just that. How to respond? He believed that they were not yet ready for this.

With his final statement (4:14–21) the claim of Paul to be their authority is decisively emphasized. The paragraph moves from the persuasive image of the father (4:15) (though ancient fathers were also authoritative teaching figures; see Ecclesiasticus 2:1; 3:1) to the coercive image of the stick (4:21), which is the alternative if love and gentleness fail. There is an irony of its own, quite different from the visible irony of the previous paragraph, in the way in which Paul has to conclude this long and carefully developed statement about the power of the cross with a threat of coercion. But it is to be noticed that the coercion is only an ultimate resort. The paragraph is designed to put the major emphasis on persuasion, pointing to Paul as the founder of the community, the bringer of the gospel, and thus both their father and the possessor of a special power, since the gospel is the vehicle of a power from beyond ordinary existence.

The call for imitating Paul (verse 16) is also in the vein of persuasion; this point leads smoothly to the question of communication between Paul and Corinth. Timothy had been sent to reinvigorate their imitation of Paul, and Paul himself is planning to come soon. The reference to his own visit, which he clearly viewed with some trepidation, called forth the threat of coercion. For coercion to appear as a final resort is natural in the nature of the case, but it is also worth noting that Paul presented his own coming as a kind of parallel to the coming of Christ, as a time of final clarification and judgment (compare the patterns of verses 4–5 and 18–19). This is no accident, but came naturally in view of the high sense of the "eschatological" vocation that he had.

Preaching and Teaching on 1 Corinthians 1—4

The Deeper Issue in This Section: Resolution or Tension

The "body" of the letter, with its reference to the expected problematic and troubling visit of Paul to Corinth, comes to a conclusion that leaves the reader with a sense of unfinished business, a lack of resolution of the tension between persuasion and coercion, between true wisdom and false wisdom. That impression results in part from the fact that much more is still to be said, in the chapters that follow, which will come to a climax in the powerful vision of the final resolution in chapter 15. To put it in other terms, the conventional distinction between the "body" of the letter and what follows it does not work very well in 1 Corinthians.

But equally important in understanding this letter, despite the "final judgment" symbolism of 4:18–21 and the final resolution imaged in chapter 15 (which, however, does not include a judgment!), is the fact that Paul was very well aware that there can be no final resolution of the tensions of earthly existence "until the Lord comes." First Corinthians, like all of Paul's letters, presents a style of faith that thrives on tension and conflict, despite the fact that the longing for resolution is also present. This note of tension pervades the whole letter (cf. 16:9, "a wide door for effective work has opened to me, and there are many adversaries"). It was one of the strengths of Paul's faith that he refused any premature resolution. One way of describing his difference with the Corinthians would be to say that he accused them of seeking a premature resolution of the tensions of existence. As he saw it, that was precisely the failure of their type of wisdom and of their understanding of the Spirit. The message of the cross means no quick resolution, no easy peace. Paul himself had to rediscover this meaning when his relations with the church at Corinth did not come to a resolution with this letter or with the visit of which he spoke here. The quest for a premature resolution of the tensions of existence has been, ever since, a principal problematic of Christian history, whether the oversimplification has come from ecstatics who stand in the line of Paul's opponents in Corinth, or from believers in rules who stand in the line of those who opposed him in Galatia.

The issue that we have tried to describe as "resolution or tension" is far from being only a matter of psychology or temperament. No doubt Paul's restless temperament played a part. (On his temperament, there is still no better sketch than John Knox, *Chapters in a Life of Paul*, chapter 6.) What is fundamentally at stake is the kind of difference it makes when God comes into the life of a person or of the church. Knowing through faith that God has come in Christ and has opened a new path to life does indeed, according to Paul, bring a newness, freedom, and joy that he can only describe in the most powerful language he can find. In faith a person's whole vision of reality is changed, and new sources of life and power (Christ and the Spirit) are at work. This side of Paul's faith had been richly taken up into the language of hymn and prayer in the church to this day.

The other side was not welcome to the Corinthians, and it has not been as fully recognized through the centuries by the church, either. For Paul, the fundamental tensions in reality were not abolished by faith. A person of faith returns to a changed reality; that is, she or he both perceives it differently and is able to draw on new powers while living in it. But this is still a reality full of paradox and tension. A closer look at main themes in the "body" of 1 Corinthians will show how Paul makes this point in different ways. In these sketches of the Spirit, wisdom, the cross, and Paul as apostle, we shall try to show some of the ways in which the themes with which Paul deals can come to expression in contemporary teaching and preaching.

Main Themes

1. The Spirit

In speaking of the Spirit Paul was speaking the language of his audience. They evidently cherished experiences of the Spirit and thought of them as distinctive signs of the new faith and life into which they had come. That is clear, even though Paul says that he could not speak to them as spiritual (3:1), deliberately reversing their own estimate of themselves. Both in chapters 2 and 3, where Paul ironically criticizes their claim to be spiritual, that is, possessed or guided by the Spirit, and in chapters 12—14, where he discusses the gifts of the Spirit, his letter makes clear the high valuation that the congregation or some important part of it put on experiences of the Spirit.

But this is also Paul's own language. He affirmed as strongly as they did that the Spirit brought new life and elevated human existence above its ordinary level. He accepted ecstatic experience as a natural sign of the Spirit's presence, just as they did. Ecstatic experience, so intense and profound that the person was lifted out of himself or herself and sensed the controlling presence of a greater power, was evidently a frequent feature of their worship. The Spirit brought a transformation of consciousness; it was an experience of a radical present. It was in speaking in tongues that this aspect of the Spirit was particularly manifest ("my spirit prays but my mind is unproductive," 14:14). Paul himself entered into all of this ("I thank God that I speak in tongues more than all of you," 14:18). It may be that he wrote in this way in part as a concession to their way of thinking, for Paul seems often to have cast his message in terms with which the audience felt at home. But that should not obscure the fact that Paul, like them, understood himself to be a Spirit-filled person.

In 1 Corinthians Paul did little to clarify just how he thought about the nature of the Spirit. Elsewhere, but infrequently, he speaks of the "Spirit of Christ" (Romans 8:9; Philippians 1:19); this phrase does not occur in 1 Corinthians, though it is of the utmost importance for Paul that the Spirit was associated with Christ. The Spirit was a presence, an immediate presence of divine power. Later Christians called the Spirit a "person"; Paul does not do this, though the Spirit certainly has personal aspects. Some people in his world thought of Spirit as an invisible fluid, and some of what Paul says can be understood in a way not very different from this. But we miss the importance of what Paul was saying when we try to resolve the theoretical question, "What was the nature of the Spirit as Paul thought about it?" The real discussion between Paul and the Corinthians was about what the Spirit did. It is easy to miss the difference between them, because when Paul wrote in the language of transformation, he sometimes spoke so strongly that it is easy to read him, too, as believing in a completed state of new being for the believer. But if we read the letter as a whole, a different picture is clear.

What Paul was opposing was a view of the Spirit's work as a finished process. Then and now, people wanted to believe that the Spirit brought them through a radical change and into a new and stable condition. That is true today of some who understand the Spirit in a charismatic way, and it is also true of others whose spiritual life is much more low-key. The longing to believe that the reality of faith is a new reality easily becomes the belief that with it one does not have to change any more.

Both in these chapters and in chapters 12—14 where he discusses the gifts of the Spirit, Paul undercuts the belief that the Spirit brings people into a finished state. For him the transition is never finished. Students of religion know how important the state of "passage" is in the religious life. We could say that Paul understood the presence of the Spirit as bringing about a continuous passage, one that is never finished in this life.

It is possible to miss this fundamental meaning of the Spirit to Paul, because he does use the language of the total transformation of life. "Those who are spiritual discern all things, and they are themselves subject to no one else's scrutiny" (2:15). This way of speaking points to the separation from the old life and the old powers that controlled life. But along with this language, Paul also uses what we have called the language of return. The Spirit does not separate us from social and cooperative responsibility. Negatively, that is shown by the criticism of self-

assertiveness and bickering (3:3–4). When we come to chapters
12 and 14, in which Paul discusses the different gifts of the Spirit,
we shall see that the strong weight lies on working and living
together in interconnectedness, in interpersonal, social harmony.
Perhaps most powerfully of all, the contrast between the Spirit
and wisdom as wrongly understood, and the cross of Christ
which is the true model for understanding the Spirit's gifts,
makes the point that one who truly understands Christ and the
mind of Christ will not be in a position of spiritual complete-
ness, but will be buffeted by the forces of life that have always
caused sorrow and suffering (4:9–13).

Paul, thus, was opposing an understanding of the Spirit that
found the clue to the Spirit in an immediate, complete experience of the present, and pointed instead to the Spirit as a guide
or lure, a divine presence that gave a direction to the complex
and unfinished life of human beings with one another. (See also
below on the cross of Christ in 1 Corinthians).

On the Spirit, see also the commentary on chapters 12 and
14.

2. Wisdom

Wisdom and the Spirit are closely related by Paul, as they
evidently were also by the Corinthians. Wisdom was one of the
principal gifts of the Spirit (2:6–13). Just as in the case of the
Spirit, Paul used language very familiar to his audience in such
a way as to challenge and alter their way of thinking about wisdom.

Wisdom was a fluid word, and its meaning varies widely
depending on the context. We can see, however, that the tensions in its meaning arise from the way in which wisdom is
directed both toward understanding the world and toward
understanding God. In an earlier time, both in the Hebrew Scriptures (the book of Proverbs) and in the Greek world (where
wisdom developed into philosophy), these two aims of wisdom were kept together. By Paul's time there were many who
found that they could not keep them together. God came to be
thought of as so remote from the world that human wisdom
could not reach to God. Wisdom could come only as a special
divine gift, a revelation. Such a separation between human wisdom and divine wisdom could be worked out in a coherent
theological and philosophical way, as it was by Paul's contemporary, the Jewish philosopher Philo of Alexandria. This thinker

pioneered the idea that revelation is a special source of knowledge, different from but coherent with philosophy. This idea later became standard among Christian theologians. Higher wisdom as revelation that represents a higher stage of insight, given by divine initiative, yet in touch with the wisdom that we can gain from studying the world, remained a principal theme of Christian theology through the centuries.

Or, the separation of wisdom from the world could depend on a direct, unanalyzed experience, interpreted only in myth. Such was the point of view of later gnosticism, and many see an early form of this mystical faith at Corinth. In this case there would be no concern to relate the special wisdom about divine mysteries to ordinary knowledge, because the world would seem to be alien from God, and wisdom would lead into a world apart. From the point of view of this kind of wisdom, the world as we ordinarily live in it was too disorderly to be a field for God's action and presence. Versions of this kind of faith are all too familiar today.

These two paths of wisdom result in very different styles of Christian faith. One kind of wisdom is understood to come from a higher realm but to be coherent with the created world—thus the created world still remains important and a place where, in one way or another, God's will is to be done. The other kind of wisdom is understood to come from a different, separated realm, unrelated or only very distantly related to the world of ordinary life. Those who seek this wisdom devalue the present world. They may not flee from it (some do), but they see little point in trying to do God's will in it. Many Christians today are in fact much closer to the second style of wisdom than they know.

What Paul says about wisdom can be taken in either direction. His strong emphasis on the irreconcilable difference between what commonly goes for wisdom, and the wisdom that is given by the Spirit, leads in the direction of a separation between the world and wisdom. Later gnostics found this a congenial reading of Paul. But the equally strong emphasis that Paul makes, that the Spirit and its gifts work for a sharing of our common life, our life in community, points in the other direction. This theme is especially strong, as we shall see, in chapters 12—14.

It is not easy to hold together the two motifs in Paul's preaching about true wisdom—one, that this wisdom comes as a gift from God to those who have faith, and the other, that it leads believers back into the ordinary, common life in which we live together. It will be a mark of our taking Paul seriously if we are able to hold these two motifs in tension, rather than putting all our interest in one of them. Unless we can hold both of them as part of our faith, we shall be putting faith and common life in two separate compartments as Christians so easily do.

3. The Cross

Paul put the theme of the cross in utter contrast with the conflicts in Corinth that, he believed, contradicted its meaning and effect. Hence he vividly painted a picture of two irreconcilable ways, the way of the cross and the way of (human) wisdom. By ordinary human standards, that is, by the standards which he believed lay behind the conflicts at Corinth, the cross appears to be foolish and weak. But in reality it is the wisdom and power of God.

We may gain a perspective on this basic theme of 1 Corinthians if we think of the cross as both the foundation and the continuing theme of a new story, a story into which Christians are drawn and in which they are guided by the same clue that can be seen in the cross of Jesus Christ at the foundational moment of the story. For Paul the story did not begin at the cross; God had intended it from the beginning. But it came to be effective in human existence at that point.

The foolishness and weakness of the cross are emphasized to drive home the point that a whole new fresh beginning has to be made in faith. New relationships, new values, new energies make up this new story. Paul was not unaware that elements from one's earlier story came into the new story of faith. In using other language he can recognize this, as in Philippians 4:8–9, where a list of virtues prized by non-Christians is held up as part of the life of faith. But here he insists on the contrast, to make the point that faith brings a total reorientation.

In 1 Corinthians Paul speaks of the cross or the death of Jesus almost entirely in the context of preaching. That is, he speaks of the cross not so much as an event in the past as the powerful center of his paradoxical message of life in death. Here the cross is a power in the present, a power that becomes actual as it is spoken and communicated. "For Christ did not send me to baptize but to proclaim the gospel, and not with eloquent wisdom, so that the cross of Christ might not be emptied of its power. For the message about the cross is foolishness to those who are perishing, but to us who are being saved it is the power of God" (1:17–18). "But we proclaim Christ crucified, a stumbling block to Jews and foolishness to Gentiles, but to those who are the called, both Jews and Greeks, Christ the power of God and the wisdom of God" (1:23–24). "For I decided to know nothing among you except Jesus Christ, and him crucified" (2:2).

These statements in their contexts set the cross over against human wisdom and success, give the criterion for the presence of the Spirit, and define the pattern of life and work of the apostle, so that the four motifs we have chosen out of these chapters are all mutually related, and all find expression in the cross. Particularly, it is by being different from (ordinary human) wisdom that the cross is understood. The key statements are all in chapters 1 and 2, where Paul says almost nothing directly about what the cross is or means, except by setting forth its contrast with ordinary wisdom and wrongly understood Spirit, and by illustrating it with his own work as apostle.

If we recall the background of wisdom in the effort to manage life, and as we say, "to stay on top of it," one meaning of the cross becomes clear—going beneath the effort to make oneself a success by the common standards of success, and going beneath the effort to gain recognition. If we recall the development of wisdom in Paul's world into an esoteric teaching that isolated the believer from others who did not have this wisdom, we see that the cross implies a strong emphasis on human solidarity. It calls us to go beyond our isolated selves and to recognize the whole community and allow ourselves to be affected by it.

It has sometimes been said that the cross means repressing or extinguishing the natural impulses of life. Paul's contrast between "flesh" and "spirit" can encourage this kind of separation between life's natural impulses and the newly channeled energy of faith. But this way of thinking badly misreads Paul. If we may translate Paul's way of speaking into psychological language, his faith was that self-transcendence is the way to life, and that this self-transcendence was made possible by the self-transcendence of God that meets us in the story of the cross of Jesus Christ. His own vocation as apostle expressed the new focusing and release of the energies of life so powerfully that it would have been impossible for him to think of the cross as a symbol for the repression of the energies of life. (See the next section.)

4. Paul as Apostle

Paul writes about being an apostle only incidentally to what he has to say about other questions, yet he finds that he has to bring in his own personal vocation and his place in the gospel process in order to clarify what the gospel itself is. This way of presenting what he is as apostle means that there are some things about his view of apostles that he does not tell us—How many apostles were there? What set them apart from others who were also witnesses to the resurrection? He does not answer these questions. Nevertheless, he does make clear what it meant to *him* to be an apostle.

As they were remembered in the later church, the apostles were *authorities*. They belonged to the first Christian generation only, and they provided a firm and correct basis for the beliefs and practices of the church. This view of the apostles was one way the church in the second century worked to establish a relatively uniform style of Christian belief and practice. It is reflected in the doctrine of apostolic succession, which holds that proper ordination can be performed only by a bishop who stands in a line running back to those bishops who were ordained by the apostles. The interpretation of the apostles as church authorities is already present in the book of Acts, where the apostles are limited to the twelve, and where Paul is not an apostle (except in Acts 14:4, 14, where Paul and Barnabas are called apostles; perhaps this different usage comes from a special source of this part of Acts).

Apostolic authority also has roots in Paul, shown in 1 Corinthians, especially in 4:19–21, the ending of the present section, where Paul appeals to his own authority to discipline the church as the final point in this major section. But for Paul, the function of an apostle as an ecclesiastical authority was a secondary one. His very irritation with the need to discipline the church reflects his desire to be doing something else.

For Paul an apostle was a figure who played a key role in response to the work of God, indeed, in the new work that God is just now carrying out. In technical language, Paul as an apostle was himself an eschatological figure, that is, a person who had a role to play in the events that lead up to the completion of God's purpose for the world and particularly for human beings. Specifically, Paul is an apostle of Christ Jesus (1:1). That means: an authorized representative or delegate of Christ, who carries on the work of Christ. In other words, it is the task, the

42

work of carrying forward what Christ was accomplishing, that marked the apostle. His primary activity as an apostle, as he understood it, was to preach and to establish new churches. "For Christ did not send me to baptize, but to proclaim the gospel" (1:17a). Though he does not discuss the point in 1 Corinthians, it appears from Romans 9—11 that the work of preaching had to be carried out as part of God's overall plan, before the end could come. (See Romans 11:13–32.)

Apostles were related to Christ by an especially close linkage. Probably all of them had "seen Jesus our Lord," that is, the risen Lord (9:1; cf. 15:3–11). An astonishing feature of Paul's account of the appearance of Christ is that he includes the appearance to him, Paul, as of equal stature with the other foundational appearances, for instance, to Peter and the twelve (15:5, 7–8). Thus he is an apostle of the same dignity as the original ones.

An apostle proclaims the same message as the church, and correspondingly, can serve as a model for the church. In one way, all believers are called to be representatives of Christ. But Paul as apostle stands in a special and close relationship to Christ as Christ's delegate or representative. This is the ground of Paul's authority, as noted above, so that the members of the congregation are not only to be like Paul (4:16; 11:1), but to do as he says (4:19–21).

What is most important for the understanding of faith is not the vexed question of authority, which lies on the surface of 1 Corinthians 1—4, but the deeper question of what it does to a person to be confronted by Christ and made Christ's apostle. Here again, Paul's letter holds together aspects of life that easily fall apart. On the one hand, the model of the cross of Christ means that the apostle is "[not] anything" (3:7), so that what Paul says of the congregation is as fully true of the apostle: "What do you have that you did not receive?" (4:7). Characteristically, this motif that would apply to every believer is heightened in his case: "For I am the least of the apostles, unfit to be called an apostle...." (15:9). As we shall see, the whole of chapter 9, where Paul's apostleship appears again, at first reading appears to be an intrusion between chapters 8 and 10 with their theme of what it is right to eat. But the chapter fits in when one sees that it aims to show how Paul as apostle sets an example of putting aside his own prerogatives and (we might say) his ego in order to be fully open to the gospel and to his work. "But I have made no use of any of these rights" (9:15); "I do it all for the sake of the gospel" (9:23). This putting aside of one's own rights is the crowning theme of chapters 8 and 10. The same point is made with powerful irony in 4:8–13, where the deprived position of the apostle is contrasted with the seeming success of the Corinthians.

But on the other hand, the very solemnity and uniqueness of being singled out by Christ as an apostle brings an immense sense of the importance and dignity of his own position. This appears not only when Paul asserts his authority, but also when he compares himself to the other apostles. In spite of his unworth, he "worked harder than any of them" (15:10; the NEB translates: "I have outdone them all"). Equally striking is the way in which he says, in 9:15, that one reason why he had not used his right (to being supported by the church) was that he would die rather than have any one deprive him of his ground for boasting. The reappearance of "boasting" in the new existence that has been transformed by the cross of Christ is most striking. Albert Schweitzer commented that the "challenge to his Apostleship had...the effect of inflaming and intensifying his self-consciousness" (*The Mysticism of Paul the Apostle*, 137).

The combination of putting one's status aside and at the same time having an intensified self-consciousness, of which Paul was so striking a model, was naturally reflected also in less intense form in the life of the members of the congregation. The friction there was not, as Paul sometimes presents it, purely the result of human failure, but arose in part from the increased sense of self-worth that the early Christians found in Christ. Paul the apostle, as a model case of this tension, provides a field of study of the combination of self-emptying and achievement that is still worth careful thought.

In our time we have seen so much of leaders who had an exaggerated sense of their "calling" that we tend to be suspicious of a vocation that claims as much authority as Paul's did, and in particular we are rightly suspicious of the tendency to project oneself into the cause that one is serving. In Paul's letters, and especially in 1 Corinthians, we find an important model for understanding the possibility of giving oneself to a cause and at the same time being self-critical about one's own actions for the sake of the cause. The cross was the model for this self-criticism. If we notice that Paul himself did not always fully embody the vision that he had, nonetheless he offers a powerful clue to what we called above the possibility of self-transcendence for the sake of a cause, in a pattern that embodies precisely the element of self-criticism that is so essential. As such, Paul's apostleship can serve as a clue for our own thinking about and testing what we understand a leader to be.

At the same time, we have to take seriously the Corinthian suspicion of Paul's claim to authority. The vital life of the community was actually being hammered out in a process of greater interaction between Paul and the members of the church than he was often aware of. To us, it seems that he was at his best when he recognized this, as he at least partly did. To him, it often appeared that the issues were too urgent to wait for an interactive solution. We shall follow this tension between Paul and the church as we read further in the letter.

Recent studies have probed the claim to imitate Paul as an apostolic model, showing how such a model can build pressure for uniformity—all should follow Paul's lead and conform to the pattern that he sets. (See Elizabeth Castelli, *Imitating Paul: A Discourse of Power*.) The assertion of power is indeed one strand in the fabric of apostleship as Paul embodied it. Before long this was the strand that was effectively remembered, as we noted at the beginning of this section. But another strand, according to which the apostle embodied both self-criticism and a concern for a multiform, varied community was more central to Paul's own self-presentation and, we believe, to the church as he interacted with it. (For a fuller presentation from this point of view, see William A. Beardslee, *Human Achievement and Divine Vocation in the Message of Paul*, 79–94.)

On "apostle," see also the commentary on chapters 4, 9, and 15:7–11.

5:1—11:1 FIRST MAIN SECTION OF "SPECIFIC ISSUES":

Questions of Personal Behavior in the Community

On the surface, these chapters at the center of the letter are rather miscellaneous. They are indeed composed of separate comments on a wide variety of topics. Paul is even responding to different sources of information. ("It is actually reported..." [5:1]; "Now concerning the matters about which you wrote..." [7:1].) Nevertheless, the emphasis here is on a series of questions about right and wrong behavior of believers—about how persons function in the community. At 11:2 the focus will shift to the life of the community itself, especially its worship.

This part of the letter, thus, is an application of the insights of chapters 1—4 to a number of urgent and difficult questions. The themes of "separation and return" and the refusal to accept a premature resolution of tension are marks of what Paul says here as before. He brings to bear on behavioral questions the faith in the cross and the faith in the Spirit that are articulated so clearly in the opening part of the "body" of the letter, even though the cross is not mentioned anywhere in these chapters, and the Spirit appears only here and there.

It is not easy to integrate basic human drives into the new vision of the fullness of life. With little exaggeration it could be said that chapters 5:1—11:1 are about food, sex, and aggression: food (8—10; it is true that only two very specific aspects of food come up here, food sacrificed to idols [chapters 8, 10], and the food that nourishes Paul [chapter 9]), sex (5; 6:12–20; 7), and aggression (6:1–11). This way of putting it has the merit of helping us to see how clearly Paul puts his new vision into dynamic interaction with basic human drives and needs.

Paul has sometimes been taken to advocate repression of these basic drives and needs. A careful reading of these chapters will show, however, that he intends to redirect them, and that his faith enlists these energies in the life of the new community. That means accepting limits and guidelines, and in a different situation these can become repressive. In Paul's case, he intends his readers to find the same immense release of energy that he had found as an apostle of Christ. That is one of the reasons why his own role reappears in this section.

5:1–13 A Community Defiled by Violation of a Taboo

Chapter 5 is not commonly read in Christian worship. At first reading it does not seem to be a promising section to stimulate contemporary reflection about the gospel. Paul is here rebuking the Corinthian church for tolerating, even boasting about, an extreme case of deviation from the norms of sexual behavior, what was in fact the violation of an incest taboo. "...a man is living with his father's wife" (5:1). Yet despite its seeming remoteness from our own concerns, it is an important section for our understanding of Paul and for the questions that it raises about the use of the Bible today.

The Plan of the Section

Chapter 5 makes an abrupt new beginning. As in 1:11, Paul starts from an oral report about the church. Yet there is a strong connection with the end of the "body" of the letter, since Paul's threatening conclusion to that section is here justified by the extreme disorder to which he now turns, and since disorder in both cases arose from people being what Paul called "arrogant" (4:18; 5:2).

The chapter is made up of two main sections: 5:1–8, which deals with the church and the man who has violated the incest taboo, and 5:9–13, which clarifies something that Paul had already written about how to get along with persons whose moral standards are different from those of the Christian community.

In the first section, the plan A, B, A' is again apparent. In 5:1–2 (A) Paul rebukes his hearers sharply for their arrogant toleration of the wrongdoer. In 5:3–5 (B) he shows how he and the church will jointly deal with the problem. Then in 5:6–8 (A')

47

he returns to their "boasting," which here receives more attention than the wrongdoing itself. The A...A' pattern also rounds off the whole chapter, as verse 13 repeats the command of verse 2 in the words of a biblical quotation: "Drive out the wicked person from among you" (Deuteronomy 17:7 and related passages).

5:1–2 The Issue at Stake: A Defiled Community

It is not clear how Paul learned of the situation. He was told about it, in contrast to learning through a letter, but he does not say by whom he was told. That he takes up the matter first of all, among the specific questions that take up most of the rest of 1 Corinthians, shows how important he felt it to be.

The wrongdoer and his offense are scarcely in the focus of Paul's thought. He simply takes them for granted. What he does concentrate on is the pollution of the community that resulted from such a presence. Thus while our attention is naturally drawn to the offender, it was the church that Paul was thinking about.

Paul had a strong sense that communities in general, including the church, were not just people grouped together, but entities that had distinctive dynamic powers running through them. More than this, the characteristic dynamic power of the Christian community, the Spirit of Christ, could be frustrated by a defiling presence, so that the community would lose its distinctive characteristic. Paul, indeed, did not quite use the language of defilement or pollution, but his use of the metaphor of the yeast or leaven that penetrates the whole, in 5:6–8, has exactly this symbolic meaning. Not only in 5:1–2, but all through 5:1–8, Paul's basic concern is to have the community expel the deviant member so that it may be purified.

According to Paul's information, the defiling power of this person had not resulted in anyone imitating him. The question of wrong sexual behavior does come up very shortly, in chapter 6, showing that this class of ethical problem was of much concern to Paul in his relation to the church in Corinth. But in this specific case, the failure of the community was clearly shown by the way in which they are "arrogant" (5:2); the episode has brought to light a trait that, he believed, marked many in the community. The fact that they can tolerate and even boast of such behavior in their midst can only be a sign that they have lost or are losing their true base.

As for the cause of the trouble, there can be little doubt that the man was living with his stepmother; Paul's exact phrase can be found in Leviticus 18:8, where the "father's wife" (as in 1 Corinthians 5:1) is distinguished from the "mother" (Leviticus 18:7). Whether the father was still alive Paul did not say, and neither is it clear whether the relationship was a formalized one, a marriage, though it seems to have been one that existed over a period of time. A marriage with one's stepmother was forbidden by Roman law, as well as by Jewish law, but that does not mean that such a marriage did not take place. It is probable that the woman was not a member of the community, though this is not said. That may be the reason why Paul does not mention the woman's responsibility for the relationship or show any concern for her as a person, in contrast to chapter 7 in which he explores the mutuality of sexual relationships. Probably the violation of the incest taboo (as we may rightly call it, despite the fact that it was almost certainly not a question of the offender's own mother) was so strongly felt to be an attack upon the father and an infringement of the father-son relationship, that no further reflection upon it seemed to be needed. Whatever else was going on, it is likely that the situation was intended just as Paul understood it, as a gesture of defiance of conventional behavior. But while we say this, we should remind ourselves that a relationship of this sort may have been more acceptable to large parts of the community than appears from the legal rules, just as is the case today in such matters.

The answers to these questions of detail are obscure, but the connection between the man and his "father's wife" was so outrageous to Paul that he did not examine it as such. The man was simply condemned and was to be put out of the church. Neither in this section nor later is anything said about intercession for him or about his possible restoration to the community. Nowhere does Paul show any concern for the woman, either.

5:3–5 A Solemn Excommunication

After his sharp attack upon the Corinthians for their failure to expel the offender, Paul goes on to show how he will be dealt with. The grammar of these three verses is obscure at several points. (It is all one sentence in Greek.) It is an awkward, passionate statement, which is not very carefully put together. Its general point is clear, but there is one difficult question that does have importance for interpretation: whether Paul in verse

3 means that he has (already) "pronounced judgment" (NRSV), or whether he has "resolved" that he (though absent) and the community *will* pronounce judgment together when they "hand this man over to Satan" (verse 5; the verb "hand...over" can have either "you" [NRSV] or "we" for a subject). The question at issue is how and to what degree the Corinthians really are to participate in the decision.

But this grammatical difficulty does not obscure the proposal that Paul makes. Certainly there is no thought of reaching a democratic decision. Paul's mind is made up, and there is no question what the decision will be. Rather, it is a question whether he is thinking of the importance of persuading the Corinthians to give their consent, so that a truly joint decision is emphasized (as C. K. Barrett thinks, *First Corinthians*, 124), or whether (as Conzelmann interprets the passage, calling it a "dynamistic ceremony") the importance of the church assembly is that this corporate context is necessary to release the dynamic, purifying, and destructive power that will transfer the offender out of the protective ambience of the church and release him to Satan (Hans Conzelmann, *First Corinthians*, 97). Paul explicitly speaks of the power of the Lord Jesus as at the center of this transfer (verse 4). The two ways of viewing the excommunication of course overlap, since the act of excommunication could not take place except through the Corinthian church. The corporate setting for the release of a dynamic power is the dominant theme, and sets this section in close relation to the understanding of community that dominates the whole chapter, that is, that human communities are not simply groups of people, but foci of trans-individual dynamic powers.

The transgression is so important that the confrontation with it cannot wait for Paul's return to Corinth. The problem must be settled at once. But Paul will be there in spirit, just as he has already "pronounced judgment" or "resolved" as if present. Again he means something stronger than what we commonly mean when we say that we will be somewhere in spirit; Paul's spirit will be a dynamic factor actually present in this transaction. One can go further; Paul's spirit will be there as a representative of Christ. The power of the Lord Jesus is even more a dynamic presence, so that the excommunication is not a mere formal change of status, but an alteration of the spiritual environment—the field of force—within which the person lives.

Paul thinks of the result as a very drastic one. This person will be delivered to Satan "for the destruction of the flesh" (verse 5), which probably means that Paul expects that he will die. This thought is similar to the one that Paul expresses in chapter 11. There he speaks of death as resulting from loss of contact with the sustaining Spirit of Christ, when the community was violated by the wrong kind of participation in the Lord's Supper ("...some have died," 11:30). The language here, distinguishing the "flesh" that will be destroyed from the "spirit" that will survive, is different from that which appears in chapter 15, where Paul insists that the new life will require a "spiritual body." This contrast is not to be pressed; it shows that we are not dealing with a precise theological vocabulary.

There is, however, a dimension of hope. Something of this errant believer's status as a person of faith will remain after this drastic procedure; indeed, Paul's language may mean that his spirit can survive only if his flesh is destroyed. The separation of flesh and spirit will take place "so that his spirit may be saved in the day of the Lord" (verse 5). The saving of the wrongdoer's spirit reminds one of 3:15, where a distinction is made between a person's work that may be lost and the person who will, even so, be saved, though "only as through fire." But chapter 5 is a far more drastic case, for nothing is said in it of any further participation by the sinner in the community. Yet, though he is separated from the human community of Christ, the power into which he came when he entered it will bring him through, broken as he is. Something like this is what Paul affirms. Though he seems to have regarded it as a case in which human beings could do nothing to help the wrongdoer (hence no reference to intercession), nonetheless, he did not believe that God acting in Christ was helpless.

5:6–8 The Danger of Pollution

By returning to the theme of purification, with which the section opened, Paul makes clear his central concern. The church is not to be the kind of group in which such a thing can happen. To make his point he uses the illustration of searching the house for traces of yeast just before the Passover, a search that becomes a metaphor for the cleansing of the community that Paul calls for. The metaphor brings into play the powerful sense of ritual purity that was associated with the Passover removal of yeast, or leaven as the older translations have it.

51

As is often the case with Paul's symbolic language, the metaphor quickly shifts, in this case from the yeast to the Passover lamb itself, which is used as a way of interpreting what the death of Christ means: "…our paschal lamb, Christ, has been sacrificed" (verse 5:7b). There does not seem to be any thought of the Lord's Supper in Paul's use of the metaphor; he turned to an already traditional interpretation of the death of Christ. This important statement points to Christ's death as a sacrifice for the whole group of believers ("us"). In passing we may note that this passage has often been used to support the view that the death of Christ actually took place at the time of the Passover (the view of the Gospel of John), rather than just before the Passover as in the Synoptics. But that question is far from Paul's mind. He uses the Passover symbolically.

The point of the shift of metaphor from the yeast to the sacrificial lamb is to move attention away from what the believer has to do (clean out the impurity) to what God in Christ has done. When that is at the center, Paul can return in the final verse to human action, with his transfer of "yeast" or leaven and "unleavened bread" to the moral responses of bad or sincere and true action. Such action, grounded in what God has done, will be the opposite of the boasting against which he protested at the start of the section.

5:9–13 Clarifying a Misunderstanding

This short section is of extraordinary interest for its reference to an earlier letter that Paul had written. We know very little about this earlier letter, the "First" Corinthians of which we know. Some scholars believe that we have a fragment of it in 2 Corinthians 6:14—7:1. It is true that that passage does not seem to belong where it now stands in 2 Corinthians, and, like the lost letter, it does strongly urge a separation between believers and nonbelievers. Yet in the 2 Corinthians passage the emphasis is on idolatry rather than on wrong sexual behavior, so this suggestion must remain only a conjecture, despite the fact that sexual wrongdoing and idolatry were traditionally very closely associated, as they are in 1 Corinthians itself.

As he now writes, Paul is clear that in his earlier letter he meant what he now says in 1 Corinthians: that it is sexual wrongdoers within the church (and other wrongdoers in the church who violate the traditional standards that Paul mentions in verse

11) from whom one must distance oneself—even to the point of not eating with them.

As for such people who are not believers, it is evident that one will have to associate with them; otherwise "you would then need to go out of the world" (verse 10). The way in which Paul says this makes clear that, although he believes that he is only reaffirming what he had said before, in Corinth his earlier letter was being interpreted as if he meant that one did indeed have to go out of the world in order to be a Christian in the way that Paul advocated.

In other words, Paul thought that he was being called on to support a view of the church as a community separated as completely as possible from the surrounding society. Such groups did exist at the time; an example is the Qumran community in Judea. But Paul, like most early Christians, intended that believers should go on functioning in the social world around the church, while at the same time they held to a distinctive ethos.

Of course, we cannot know how he expressed himself in his earlier letter. Many scholars hold that he had not yet clearly seen the distinction that he now makes. However that may be, his position here is consistent with what he says elsewhere in 1 Corinthians, as in chapter 10, where he permits church members to eat with unbelievers who, unless they are Jews, will automatically be "idolaters" (10:27).

The aspect of judgment, which has been so prominent in the whole chapter, links this section with the deeper intention of what precedes. One can leave the judgment of outsiders to God, but within the church, Christians are to judge. Not associating with wrongdoers is an important part of the judgment upon them. This point is reinforced by the somber concluding command to drive out the wicked person, which is taken from Deuteronomy 17:7, a passage that comes at the end of a section dealing with the stoning to death of a Hebrew who had deviated by worshiping other gods.

Preaching and Teaching on 1 Corinthians 5

Limits to Responsible Freedom

This chapter is not one of those where Paul allows a degree of leeway to the congregation or its individual members. He speaks with authority. It was self-evident to Paul that the action in question was thoroughly wrong and could only be condemned. In fact, it is likely that to the person who was living with his father's wife, the act did appeal in part precisely because it involved a flaunting of conventional standards.

Paul was far more aware than most men and women of his time that there are varieties of ways of establishing a network of relationships within which human beings could live. He stood at the intersection of three ways—the Jewish, the "Greek," and the emerging Christian. And he could to some extent move from one to another and shift his ways of behaving ("To those outside the law I became as one outside the law…" [9:21]).

Nevertheless, there were limits within which the diversity of human patterns of life could exist. And the man of chapter 5 had totally exceeded these limits.

We should not pass over Paul's outrage at what he saw as a transgression of a natural taboo without pointing out that though all cultures have incest taboos, the limits of forbidden relationship vary greatly. It was of no concern to Paul that there are cultures—and presumably there were then, too—in which it is an obligation, at times, to marry one's (deceased) father's wife. This is the case in some African cultures. Usually it is a brother who assumes the responsibility of marrying and caring for the bereaved woman. This is the regular way in which the surviving wives are cared for in some polygamous cultures. There is a parallel in the obligation to marry the deceased brother's wife of the so-called Levirate law (Deuteronomy 25:5–10). But in some groups, if there is no brother, it is the responsibility of a son to marry the father's wife or wives. The reason for pointing out this variety is that for us today, the interaction among cultures of varying standards is a more complex question by far than it was in Paul's time. It will not necessarily do simply to apply the biblical standard even to such a fundamental question as incest.

In the actual case of African polygamous cultures, most of the "mainline" churches have insisted that Western, "Christian" standards are the only possibility for African Christians, while a number of the African churches of African origin have approached the question of marriage and incest with an open mind, and have held that local custom may find its way into the church. While this may seem like a rather esoteric example, it is presented here to help the reader reflect on the complexity of the problem of drawing connections between Scripture and contemporary life. Paul thought that the behavior he was condemning was forbidden by some universal human consensus, while these limits are far more culturally determined than biblical writers realized.

That does not mean that anything goes! Within the situation there was a right and a wrong, as Paul rightly saw. In many other cases he also saw that the right is not discerned simply by applying a rule. Here it was clear to him that the rule was a good guide. He was probably right, though our discussion has tried to set this situation in a wider framework. He was thoroughly right that there are always limits to responsible freedom, and the individual person cannot find these limits in isolation. God's point of view, mediated by the Spirit, can direct believers as they seek for it together, even though our perception of and response to God's leading is always imperfect.

The Community as a Field of Force

As we have seen, it was more important to Paul for the Corinthians to understand what their community was like than it was to examine in detail the wrongdoing. What is most important to think about is not the specific standard of behavior, but the insight that a Christian community is not simply a gathering of separate people, but that it is a field of force, and that this force can be interrupted or destroyed if a counterforce is introduced into it. The force within the community was the Spirit, about which Paul had written earlier, and to which he will return in chapters 12 and 14. The counterforce is not defined, but this whole section of the letter is full of references to polluting or destructive forces, mostly sexual or idolatrous.

As so often in 1 Corinthians, the modern preacher or teacher who is interpreting this chapter will have to probe deeper than the specific question at issue. In what way can we think of our churches as fields of force, and especially as fields of force in which the negative forces are in principle overcome but still threaten to reassert themselves? What compels us to re-form the question is the fact that the power of Christ is not easily defined so narrowly with respect to Christian worship as Paul could do. That is still the focus; but we recognize Christ at work in other ways as well. The conflict between the field of force of the Spirit or the living Christ and the negative powers was for Paul concentrated in the life of the Christian community. Perhaps one way of viewing the shift to our time is that we have to see this struggle as a small-scale representation of a contest that is going on all about us.

For instance, we could not today responsibly approach the question of sexual abuse of children solely within the circle of the church. Destructive forces such as patriarchal domination and the dissociation of body and spirit that have allowed some people to ignore or excuse bodily actions are powers present in the church as well as outside it. And the healing powers such as confronting the evil, acknowledging it, and granting forgiveness are the work of the Spirit of Christ, but also are at work without being recognized by this name.

6:1–20 Two Issues that Test the Community: Litigation and Wrong Sexual Behavior

6:1–11 A Community Losing Sight of Its Basis

With chapter 6 there is an abrupt change of subject, though as we shall see, there is far more connection to what preceded and to what follows than appears on first reading. We move from the highly charged atmosphere of a cultic ceremony of excommunication to the very daily and ordinary problem of disputes between members of the Corinthian community, disputes that lead to lawsuits litigated before the same courts that any citizen of Corinth would use.

Thus the theme of judging links this discussion to what has gone before, and both sections deal with the responsibility that the church is to take for all the actions of its members. In both cases the question of judging is set in the framework of the boundaries of the community. That is, both issues were illustrations of the need to establish a sharp separation between the Christian group and those outside it. It is worth noting that Jewish communities, too, had courts of their own to decide disputes among members.

Paul's treatment of this issue is a masterpiece of scornful writing, and the embedding of this question, which at first glance seems of little importance for faith, in the context of the

intensely felt questions of sexual behavior, sets the stage for
Paul's demonstration of how important in fact the question is.
In Greek the first word of the chapter is the challenging word,
"dare," that is, "...do you dare to?... ," which shows at once
how far away from the proper way of acting Paul claims that
these disputes are.

The sacred power of the community that was to be shown
in the process of excommunication just discussed appears in
different form when Paul affirms an already traditional belief
that "the saints will judge the world" (verse 2; cf. Matthew 19:28)
and also "angels" (verse 3). Those to whom such a transcendent privilege of judgment has been granted by their associa-
tion with Christ have no business putting their disputes before
nonbelieving judges. This is especially so because the disputes,
which do not engage the new faith, are "trivial cases" (verse 2).
They deal with "this life" (verse 3, RSV; NRSV "ordinary matters"), which is thereby sharply contrasted with the new life
into which they have entered (cf. 7:29–31, which also relativizes
the concerns of this life by setting them in the framework of the
coming age). This theme is another expression of Paul's basic
conviction that the community of believers was animated by a
different "field of force," as we have called it, from that which
animated society at large.

That the believing community would share in the judgment
or ruling of the world was already affirmed in Jewish
eschatological faith (cf. Daniel 7:27); here in 1 Corinthians the
believers' participation is made possible by their belonging to
Christ. The implication, of course, is that such a community
must have members who are competent to judge any daily disputes that arise—rather than having the disputants refer them
to nonbelieving judges, those who "have no standing in the
church" (verse 4; this verse can also, less probably, be understood as it was in the KJV, as a command to lay the problems
before the humblest ["least esteemed"] members of the community).

Paul goes further in insisting that to have such disputes at
all is a sign that something is badly awry. Why do they not let
the matter at issue go? Instead, they are engaged in defrauding
their own fellow believers! This is the climax of his attack. The
point that the correct way within the community is to refrain
from insisting on one's own rights points forward to chapter
13, especially 13:5. The reader cannot help being reminded of

Jesus' words about allowing oneself to be deprived, in Matthew 5:38–42, but we cannot tell whether Paul had these words in mind.

Their behavior in these disputes casts doubt on the nature of their sharing of the life of faith. It is precisely a sign of their lack of justice. And those who are wrongdoers cannot inherit the coming kingdom of God. This presumably traditional statement leads into a typical list of vices, which is prefaced by "wrongdoers," and which as usual with Paul includes a number of terms that express people setting themselves against one another. This list, however, is marked by a larger than usual number of terms for wrong sexual behavior. They are included to link the wrong behavior of 6:1–11 with the more obviously wrong sexual behavior of chapter 5 and of 6:12–20. The list also serves the purpose of reinforcing the repeated point that there is a decisive line between the community and those outside it.

Those who practice the vices of this rather traditional list are excluded from the kingdom of God; the church, on the other hand, has been purified by baptism ("you were washed," verse 11), and is not to manifest any of these traits. Not all outsiders actually practiced such vices, of course, and Paul asserts that only "some" (verse 11) of the Corinthian Christians had done so. The main point is that Paul insists that a standard of moral behavior is the mark of the Spirit-filled community that has been created by the death of Christ. Such behavior will be the outcome of the new field of force within which they live. At the same time, it is important for us to remember that the actual standards of behavior that are here criticized were not uniquely criticized by Paul or by Christians. The vices are traditional.

The list of vices includes a strong component of sexual sins, as well as idolatry, which was already associated with sexual misconduct in the Old Testament, and sins of theft and self-indulgence. "Fornicators" (verse 9) includes a wide range of wrong sexual behavior. "Male prostitutes, sodomites" (verse 9) translates two Greek words that have usually been taken to mean those who practice passive and active male homosexual acts. Since this question is important for present-day ethics, it should be noted that an able scholar has recently challenged these translations, and holds that Paul was speaking more generally, and not of homosexual acts. This scholar would translate the first Greek word (*malakoi*) as "unrestrained" or "wanton," and the second (*arsenokoitai*) as "male prostitutes." (John

Boswell, *Christianity, Social Tolerance, and Homosexuality*, 106–107
and Appendix 1.) This proposal rightly draws attention to the
fact that the first of the words that Paul uses was a common one
with a wide range of meaning, while the second was an unusual one and therefore obscure. Boswell is right that Paul was
not focusing on homosexuality (he drew this list from tradition), but he has gone beyond the evidence in claiming that this
passage does not deal with it at all. (See Robin Scroggs, *The
New Testament and Homosexuality*.)

Paul did, indeed, in a way quite in keeping with his tradition, include (male) homosexual acts among the things condemned in this list of vices (his only other reference to homosexuality is Romans 1:26–27). Paul's view is part of what we
bring to the subject, but it can be only one component in contemporary understanding of this question. As in many other of
the concrete issues in 1 Corinthians, we would impose an un-
workable rigidity if we tried to make his judgments permanent
rules for the guidance of Christians. This is all the more the case
in the present instance where a detailed analysis of vices was
far from Paul's intention. He used the list to highlight the in-
sider-outsider contrast. Not literally applicable in its own day
(since the outside world was not as vicious as Paul painted it,
and the inner world of the church was not as perfect), the list is
to be taken seriously not for its details but for its reminder that
entry into the Christian community brings a person into a new
community with a new ethos.

This section closes on this note: God's coming to you has
brought about a break with dehumanizing practices.

The theme of difference from the surrounding community
needs to be held in contrast to the corresponding theme of an
open, varied community, which is fundamental for Paul. In
many ways Paul was very open: Jews and Greeks, slaves and
free, men and women were all to be full participants in the community (though he did not realize what full participation of
women would be). He had not considered that gay and lesbian
people, too, were to be included in an open community. He did
not understand what a homosexual orientation was, as no one
did at the time. Nor had he thought very much about it. The
question of homosexuality comes up only in passing as something Paul took for granted. Far more important for our thinking is Paul's deep conviction that the community of Christ is
open to a wide variety of people. Today we will include gay

and lesbian people in the open community of the church, drawing on this deeper theme of 1 Corinthians. (See the fine discussion in Victor P. Furnish, *The Moral Teaching of Paul*, chapter 3.)

6:12–20 The Body Belongs to Christ

The list of vices has paved the way for a return to the question of sexual behavior. Here as in chapter 5 Paul is arguing against a Corinthian position. It is difficult to know how far he is arguing against what some in the church were actually practicing, or whether he is using his illustration as a way of reducing to absurdity what some of them were theoretically claiming about their bodily freedom.

The discussion of relations with prostitutes begins with a quotation from Corinth: "All things are lawful for me" (verse 12). Paul did not disagree with this saying, but he firmly insisted that for those who believe, the conclusions that were being drawn from this freedom were wholly wrong. A person is not an isolated individual, but is drawn into a network of relations that are an essential part of the constitution of his or her selfhood. These relations move in two directions: on the one hand, to the community of which one is a part, and on the other, to Christ, the Spirit, and God. In the closely related section on food offered to idols (chapters 8 and 10), the network of human relationships in the community is a focus of attention. Here, on the other hand, it is the contrast between the relations to God, the Spirit, and Christ, on the one hand, and the relations with a prostitute, on the other, that forms the discussion.

What Paul was opposing was the claim that the spiritual aspect of the human person was so sharply separated from its fleshly, bodily container that what went on in the body did not affect the spirit. Later Paul will agree that food is indifferent (chapters 8 and 10). To that degree he can be seen as in agreement with the Corinthian claims. The maxim that "Food is meant for the stomach, and the stomach for food" (verse 13), is probably also a quotation from Corinth. The inference was that other bodily acts were indifferent in the same way. Paul makes his case with the distinction between "stomach" and "body." The body is not merely a physical organism; it is a way of speaking about the self. And the body—the whole self—is not a self-sufficient entity, but derives its nature from the Christ to whom it is related. That bodies of believers are "members of Christ" (verse 15) makes this point. With this vision of what a person is, it is clear that the instrumental use of the body in the impersonal relation with a prostitute is a misuse of the body. The reference to the body as a "temple" (verse 19) ties in with the image of the temple in 3:16–17; the Spirit is within you, and not at a distance from the body.

Preaching and Teaching on 1 Corinthians 6

It is ironic that most of the church's teaching has held that the second half of chapter 6 is permanently valid teaching, while the first half, which deals with lawsuits, does not have to be taken literally. But it is not surprising that it has worked out this way. Part of the reason for putting the discussion of lawsuits between two questions of sexual behavior was to make the point that the sort of aggressive efforts to get the better of other believers was just as bad as the much more widely condemned sexual misbehavior. And through the centuries Christians have much more easily accepted disputatious and grasping behavior by members of the church than they have accepted sexual misconduct.

To put it differently, Paul had a vision of a sharply distinct community of faith, yet one that also interacted with the surrounding society not only in the area of earning a living, but also in marriages with nonbelievers (7:12–16) and in social friendships (10:27). Such a balance is hard to maintain. It is easier to draw vague lines or else to withdraw much more sharply.

Thus in preaching or teaching from this chapter, it is important to press to the deeper issue: what is the nature and style of the Christian community? More important than the specific behavior condemned is the vision and reach toward a knowledge of our interconnectedness as believers, yet an interconnectedness that, as Paul saw, does not cut us off from others, but rather keeps us open toward them.

On the one hand, such an awareness, while it will not do away with the necessity for the legal profession, will open the path to a mutual trust and support even in cases of conflict. We must hold this vision even in times of tension and conflict, which are indeed a constant part of our interrelatedness; this vision can open the way to a fresh and more open way of resolving conflict.

A similar approach applies to the second half of the chapter. Christian faith will always call for a profound sense of responsibility in sexual behavior. The positive side of this is presented by Paul in chapter 7. Here the negative side is based on the intimate and transforming relationship between the believer and Christ, which prevents one from treating the body as a mere instrument. Again, it is the relatedness of the human person as a whole being that prevents one's act from being judged as one's private business.

The teacher or preacher who plans to speak about the specific subject of this section, prostitution, will consider an aspect of the subject that does not enter Paul's discussion: What does it mean to be a prostitute? Further, we should note that Paul's discussion presents sexual questions primarily from the point of view of the male, in terms of an opposition between marriage and relations with prostitutes. A whole range of relationships that the church, like all people in our culture, has to understand, do not appear at all in Paul's discussion. The many types of relationships that exist between women and men today should not be forced into Paul's model.

What Paul offers for the church today, for both issues of the chapter, is not specific patterns of behavior that can be directly adopted, but a vision of responsibilities and of a common life in interconnectedness. The interwoven character of human life leads on the one hand from the individual to the community of faith, so that freedom "builds up" that community and is not an exercise of individual self-assertion; on the other hand, that interconnectedness leads also toward God in Christ. This latter is a transforming relationship, which enables and opens the way to an awareness of oneself as a vehicle for the work of God.

7:1–40 Marriage and the Roles of Men and Women

Paul's Approach to Marriage

Chapter 7 deals with marriage. Since the modern reader lives in a world in which the stability of marriage is under great pressure, we tend to read this chapter for its emphasis on the permanence of marriage, and tend to look in it for what it says about the importance of marriage and the weight of one's commitment to it. It is natural that readers in the church, feeling marriage threatened, should see in the Bible an ally and aid in their search for grounds and arguments in favor of lasting marriage.

Nevertheless, this common approach to chapter 7 tends to turn Paul's statements upside down. To put it simply, we want to hear that marriage is *important*. As against the forces in our society that lead to the instability of marriage, contemporary Christian readers look for statements about the value of marriage to the personal wholeness or fulfillment of the person, or to the empowering of marriage as a Christian vocation. We want to hear Paul saying in chapter 7, "Stay married because marriage is so important."

Put this way, the contrast between Paul and our world immediately becomes evident. Paul does indeed say, "Stay married," but, he says, do so precisely because marriage is *not* important. Though there is much else in the chapter besides the theme of permanence in marriage, the task of appropriating Paul's thought for our time is best thrown into focus by this difference between what we want him to say in order to buttress our understanding of marriage and what he actually does say. The whole chapter is strikingly unmodern, and yet this very contrast with our usual assumptions may open the way for new insight.

Another general comment will guide us toward the chapter. Just as instructive in chapter 7 as Paul's treatment of specific issues is his effort to bring together two ways of seeing the problems in hand. On the one hand, he strove to lay before his readers a vision of the life of faith; it was, of course, in this vision that marriage was so drastically relativized. On the other, he tried to deal both compassionately and honestly with human beings whose lives were far from representing the vision. So put, Paul's procedure may sound commonplace, and indeed it does share those traits with good pastoral concern elsewhere. But what is specially worth noting here is the interaction between two ways of grasping the issues. It is too often thought that the vision of life that a person of faith is trying to communicate is fixed, and given by sources quite different from the concrete persons addressed. Paul himself may have sometimes thought about his pastoral concerns in that way. But when we see him actually at work, we see how the vision and the actual persons with their problems deeply interact with each other.

Not only is the concrete advice tempered by the limits of the situation to which it is addressed, but the vision itself is modified by the "counseling situation." The complex subject of the relations between men and women in marriage and in the church is an illustration of this interaction between concrete persons and an encompassing vision of a new reality. The equality for men and women toward which Paul moved was not given simply by his vision, but arose as well from the actions and hopes and leadership of women in the church, and from the impact of the wider society in which, for instance, women clergy functioned in some religious groups such as that of Isis.

In another way the chapter calls for special attention, as a prime illustration of a process evident throughout the letter. The modern reader tends to look for Paul's answers. The presupposition is that if the New Testament is going to be important, it will have to be because it offers answers to problems. Approached in this way, the chapter does offer many "answers," many specific decisions about questions of marriage. It was in fact written in reply to some questions that the Corinthians had asked (7:1; cf. 7:25). But once again, our way of asking the question may lead us to miss the balance, in Paul's approach to concrete issues, between giving answers and putting the responsibility for decision in the hands of the persons concerned. He did not give nearly the amount of "answers" that we expect. If one of the original readers of the letter came to it with the question, "Should I get married?" he or she would have found Paul saying, "You have to decide that for yourself." Occasions for such decision can be seen, for instance, in 1 Corinthians 7:5, 9, (15), 21 (see discussion below), 36, 39. Of course, the scope for decision is set by a strong framework of given standards, as in 7:2, 10–11, 17, 39. But the reader, ancient or modern, who goes to 1 Corinthians 7 for answers will miss the way in which Paul, for all his passionate sense of his own authority as well as his sense of the authority of the tradition that he had received, worked toward putting the responsibility for choice in the hands of the persons who actually had to deal with the problem.

Chapter 7 works its way through a series of problems, with some overlapping and (for us) some occasional obscurity about just what the problem was. In the course of dealing with these concrete issues, Paul twice interrupted his presentation by digressions that point to what was more fundamental to him than the specific issues his hearers had raised. It is these two interruptions of the main surface thread of the discourse (7:17–24, 29–31) that make clear how and why Paul relativized marriage. As noted above, in contrast to most modern Christian readers who want him to sustain marriage because it is important, Paul regarded marriage as a lesser issue.

Both Paul and the readers particularly addressed in this chapter believed that it was possible for life to be transformed radically. But they differed on what that transformation was to be. The fundamental issue that shapes his comments on marriage, then, is the question of how life may be radically transformed. In other terms, it was Paul's hope, his eschatological vision, that came to expression in these two digressions, for his vision of how life may be radically transformed was eschatological; he awaited the radical transformation at the end, while at the same time already beginning to participate in it. He understood some of his hearers to believe that the transformation was already fully in place, or (if they were imaging themselves less eschatologically) that their access to spiritual power separated them from the old forms of life.

The Outline of the Chapter

The matters dealt with in chapter 7 are as follows: (1) is sexual intercourse right at all? (verses 1–7); (2) it is preferable to remain unmarried, but once undertaken, marriage is to be permanent; an exception is permitted in the case of a marriage to a non-Christian partner who wishes to end the marriage (verses 8–16); (3) the advice to remain in whatever state one is in is illustrated by means of the conditions of being a Jew or a non-Jew and of being a slave or a free person (this is the first digression [verses 17–24]); (4) the virgins and specifically the "betrothed" and those betrothed to virgins are advised that if they do marry it is not a sin (this section is broken apart by the second and major digression on how to live in expectation of radical transformation, or the coming of the end [verses 25–37, with the digression in verses 29–31]); (5) a final note advises, but does not command, widows that they will be better off not to remarry (verses 39–40).

7:1–7 Sexual Relations in Marriage

The opening question, whether sexual intercourse is right at all, comes from the letter that the church or a group of its members had written to Paul. The same opening phrase, "Now concerning... ," begins the discussion of the "virgins" in verse 25, which is thus probably an answer to another question of the church. It is very likely that other issues in the chapter were also raised by the Corinthian letter, but we cannot know how detailed it was. Probably from this point on throughout the rest of the letter, many of the topics discussed were suggested by the letter that Paul had received. This is suggested by the repeated "Now concerning..." (7:1, where their letter is mentioned, 25; 8:1; 12:1; 16:1, 12). Yet the shift between chapters 6 and 7 to a new focus on the letter from Corinth is combined with a continuity of theme, sexual behavior, that connects this chapter with 6:12–20 and thus with chapters 5 and 6.

It is surprising that Paul had to counsel against both lax standards (6:12–20) and highly ascetic standards of sexual behavior (in much of chapter 7). Most students conclude that in Corinth there were two ways of responding to a powerful faith in the transformation of life by contact with the spiritual, nonmaterial realm. One group believed that since they had become spiritual it was of little importance what they did with their bodies. Paul responded to this position in 6:12–20. The other group, to which Paul spoke in chapter 7, held that since the body is a lower reality, physical things and especially sex were to be avoided as much as possible. These two perspectives continued into gnosticism as it developed, and even though contemporary spirit-oriented groups tend strongly in the second direction, there is ample evidence, even in the newspapers, that these are two perennial alternatives if the body is devalued.

The opening statement, "It is well for a man not to touch a woman," seems to have been a quotation from the Corinthian letter. Paul himself was not unsympathetic to this point of view. (See verses 8–9, 26, 39–40.) But he first answers from the opposite side, saying that the normal course of events is for men and women to be married and in marriage to have sexual intercourse regularly. Once married, a person does not have the freedom to refrain, because the partner's need for sex overrules any personal preference for abstinence that one might have. This advice recognizes the sexual needs of both men and women equally. Perhaps this advice pressed more heavily on some of the women than on most of the men, since it may be that it was mainly women who were led to abstain from sexual intercourse in order to be more open to the Spirit. But the advice was directed to both sexes. It was directed against persons in the church who were trying to spiritualize Christian existence to the point where the need for sex would not function. Paul had no sympathy for such a transformation of existence; if one has a gift for celibacy, as will soon appear, it *precedes* and does not follow the transformation of existence by Christian faith. Note, however, that Paul did not oppose this competing, celibate, vision with any romantic picture of love or even with a view of marriage as personal fulfillment. Nothing is said about companionship, though this is implied by the mutual understanding of each other's needs (see also 11:11), and nothing is said about children as the purpose of sex. Children are of course presupposed (verse 14), but Paul seems to have had little interest in them, in contrast to the usual Jewish and pagan writing about marriage. To some extent his lack of interest in children probably sprang from his faith that the end was near, though other factors may have contributed. No, marriage is simply the way in which human persons come together as sexual beings. Nowhere in this chapter does Paul mention the word love. His was a thoroughly nonromantic view of marriage.

Having said this, we must remember that the focus falls on sexual relations because that was what the Corinthians had asked about. What Paul says does not by any means presuppose a "mechanical" view of sex. Rather he presupposes that married couples, like all believers, will approach each other with mutual consideration. (See Victor P. Furnish, *The Moral Teaching of Paul*, chapter 2.)

Paul's insistence that each partner must respect the sexual needs of the other was not at all intended as permission to use force. The mutual respect to which Furnish alludes is presupposed. Violence in marriage is not in view anywhere in the chapter. Since it is a contemporary issue, a modern interpreter must make clear that Paul in no way condones such violence.

Given the very practical starting point, the first section is all the more remarkable for the thorough equality between the partners that Paul set forth. Though the opening (probably quoted) statement had been framed in terms of the man, Paul's answer dealt equally with men and women as sexual beings, each of whom is to ask for and to give sexual mutuality. The move toward a thoroughgoing equality of the sexes was not completely worked out in the chapter. For instance, in verse 27 the question is addressed to the male: "Are you bound to a wife?" And the section on the fiancées or virgins (verses 36–

38) is cast purely in terms of decision by the man. Nevertheless, both here and later in the chapter, Paul goes out of his way to make clear that the "one body" (6:16) of marriage is a meeting of two equal human beings. The striking statement of Galatians 3:28 could not be used here: "there is no longer male and female; for all of you are one in Christ Jesus"; for in this context Paul wanted to emphasize the fact that in Christ there are indeed differentiations between male and female that still continue to be functional in marriage. However, the vision of a new reality in which existing social role models for men and women were transcended was a marked feature of early Christianity and here of Paul. Just as Paul translated the vision of "no longer male and female" into an acceptance of women as leaders in the church (for instance, the Prisca of "Aquila and Prisca" [16:19], and elsewhere), so here he translated it into a recognition of the full equality of both sexes precisely as sexual beings.

His recognition of equality was not as full as he thought, in all probability. Women who were discovering new freedom to function in new ways in the church were probably important if not predominant among those who wished to abstain from traditional marriage roles in order to be free for their new functions. Then as now it was difficult for men to see that women could really find fulfillment in other roles than marriage. The weight of his admonition to fulfill the traditional role may well have fallen most heavily on them.

Paul did allow that for a fixed period, by mutual consent, a couple might practice abstinence in order to devote themselves (intensively) to prayer. Clearly all couples are expected to engage deeply in prayer in any case, so we have here a type of special act of personal devotion. Whether this provision reflects a sense that there is something defiling about sex that is antithetical to prayer has been much discussed. Paul does not say this. He may have been thinking of it simply as a distraction.

The section closes with the other side of the picture: "I wish that all were as I myself am" (that is, unmarried, verse 7). It is unprofitable to speculate whether Paul was a widower. He affirms that though marriage is usual and thoroughly acceptable, it is not the best way. But Paul made clear that the choice of the unmarried way was not an opportunity to achieve a higher spiritual level. It is simply a matter of whether one has the gift for it;

the gift, that is, of not being driven by sexual desire. This gift is not specially associated with Christian faith. It is not part of the radical transformation of life. The statement in verse 7 that each has his or her special gift does not mean that the need for sexual activity is a gift corresponding to the gift of freedom from this need. On the contrary, a person who does not have the gift of continence and hence marries will find that some other gift enables her or him to serve Christ in some other way.

7:8–16 The Unmarried and Widows; Mixed Marriages

This remark leads to the next section, which gives advice to the unmarried and widows, to the married, and to the "rest" (verse 12), who turn out to be persons whose spouses are not Christians. The first group, the unmarried and the widows, may marry if they need to. The married, in accord with one of Paul's few citations of a saying of Jesus (Mark 10:11–12 and parallels) are to stay married. There is no suggestion that Paul knew of the exception, that divorce was permissible in case of unchastity (Matthew 5:32). Jesus' command against divorce had probably been intended as a protection of the wife, whose position and rights were sharply limited. (See Herbert Braun, *Jesus of Nazareth: The Man and His Time*, 79.) Paul did not seem to have had this point in mind; he cited the saying simply on the authority of the Lord. If this is correct, it is all the more remarkable that a powerful eschatological vision of the transformation of existence worked independently both in the case of Jesus and in that of Paul, to alter an existing social inequality toward fuller recognition of both members of a marriage as fully responsible for and in it.

It is striking that Paul's opposition to divorce in verses 10–11 is directed primarily to women who wish divorce or separation (the latter Paul grudgingly allows). Here is another indication that women were finding new freedom in the new roles that the church opened to them.

We can comment that through the centuries the church has usually tried to follow the lead of this chapter and make divorce very difficult. It is easy to see why. But this legalistic approach to marriage has made life harsh for many couples, and today it is increasingly recognized that fixed rules will not work. As in Paul's Corinth, today the roles of men and women are not rigidly defined by society, and the church faces new tasks in reimagining the patterns of marriage.

The third group addressed in this section, members of the community whose spouses are not Christians, poses a new problem. Since the powers of life are focused in the community, and yet since sex, as the focal linking power between two persons and the powers at work in their lives, is itself so powerful a force, the question arises whether these powers are on a collision course, so to speak, so that once again abstinence or abandonment of the marriage is indicated. No, Paul answered, the powers that are at work in the believer are stronger than those at work in the nonbeliever. The marriage is to continue.

Paul strengthened his position by an odd reference to the children, the only reference to children in the chapter. They are "holy," but would be "unclean" if it were not the case that the power at work in the community flowed into them. Numerous attempts have been made to draw some conclusions about baptism from these verses (13–14). But nothing is said about baptism. It is said only that a power is at work with the result that the unbelieving partner is "made holy" (verse 14) and the children are "holy." We would be wrong to try to resolve this deep sense of the almost physical power of holiness into an interpretation of personal faith that is congenial to us. It is one of the places where Paul shows a wider sense of the mysterious power of God's work than can be brought into focus in his words about faith. To grapple with the awareness of unresolved mystery at the edge of faith is a perennial task of the believer.

But Paul returns to the personal with the remark that if the unbelieving partner wishes to dissolve the marriage, he or she is to be let go in "peace" (verse 15). Further, he says that "in such a case the brother or sister is not bound" (verse 15), which is a clear indication that it would be possible for the believing partner to marry again. The section closes with a further thought about such "mixed" marriages—perhaps the husband or wife may come to believe in Christ. This is not a promise, but it is an added reason why such marriages are to continue. Elsewhere, of course, he advised or perhaps commanded that such marriages with nonbelievers should not be contracted (verse 39, as it is probably to be interpreted). But of course these "mixed" marriages might easily come into existence when one of the spouses becomes a believer. When they do exist, they are to be dealt with as shown above.

70

7:17–24 The Transformation of Life and the Stability of Social Patterns

The third section of the chapter is a digression from the theme of marriage. Its basic point is to stay in the state you are in, whether as Jew or non-Jew, slave or free; and, correspondingly, whether married or unmarried. One of these comparisons is loaded with sacred meaning (the comparison between Jew and non-Jew). In this context, marriage has a similar sense of awe about it, not that marriage was in any way sacramental in Paul's thought, but it was a divinely ordered way of regulating both a fundamental human relationship and an immensely powerful urge. In both the Jewish/non-Jewish and the married/unmarried cases, it is clear that the advice to remain in one's state when called to be a believer is more than advice. It is at least close to a command—though with openness in the case of the unmarried. We know from Galatians how strongly Paul urged that the given line between Jews and non-Jews should not be infringed by non-Jews receiving circumcision, even though the line had in one sense been erased by faith in Christ (Galatians 2:1–10; 5:2; cf. 3:28).

From the earlier part of 1 Corinthians 7 it is clear that the state of marriage is not as inflexible, since the unmarried may marry. The third area of comparison, the distinction between free persons and slaves, is a thoroughly secular area. Probably the advice to the slave not to take freedom if she or he had the opportunity is not as strong a command as in the other two cases. (Verse 21 is probably correctly translated in the NRSV: "Even if you can gain your freedom, make use of your present condition now more than ever." However, the Greek is obscure, and some translators, as in the RSV, make it read in the opposite way: "… if you can gain your freedom, avail yourself of the opportunity.")

But all three areas make clear that the transformation of life that Paul preached was not expected to transform these social patterns. In no way could Paul have more clearly made the point that marriage is drastically relativized by the life in the new community than by comparing marriage or nonmarriage to Jew or non-Jew and slave or free. Human existence within these patterns was altered by Christ, and thereby the functioning of the patterns was changed. But as Paul understood it, the framework within which human beings were related was not changed. This contrast is an oversimplification, though it makes Paul's

71

point. When the relations within the structure are changed as radically as they would be by recognizing the equality of the sexes as fully as Paul did, the structure of marriage will change also, though Paul did not see this clearly. The way in which, in another generation or two, most parts of the church moved back into a more traditional male-dominated pattern of marriage shows this to be the case; the Pauline pattern was an unstable one, pulled in two ways. Something of the same sort could also be said about the other two illustrations that he uses.

But these sociological reflections about such patterns of relationship should not turn attention away from Paul's main point. He was affirming that a person of faith can, indeed must, bring into the structural relationships of society a new stance, a new way of entering into those relationships, which is far more important than the relationships themselves. And this new stance is no mere individual faith, but the life of a new community, the community of faith, a new social structure that intersects, so to speak, with the existing ones.

Some of the Corinthians, especially some of the women, expected the new life in faith to bring about a greater change in the patterns of marriage. When we consider how patriarchal marriage was at the time, we have to acknowledge that though Paul was moving in the direction of equality of the sexes in marriage, he did not see the inequalities as clearly as he could have.

7:25–35 Freedom Within Your Condition

The next part of the chapter (verses 25–35) returns to the list of types of marriage situations, but it breaks off again before the problems of the specific type of person are clarified, with another digression that urges people to remain in the state they are in. Probably in response to a question in their letter, Paul begins to write about "virgins." As in verse 12, he specifically notes in verse 25 that he is giving his own (not "the Lord's") opinion. His opinion is that those who have never married will do better not to marry. This opinion, however, is generalized to include both the married and the unmarried: both are to remain as they are. However, he goes on to say that marrying is not a sin.

This time Paul probes more deeply into his reasons: it is not an ordinary time, but one of impending "crisis," and a time in which married persons will have troubles that will distract them from the service of the Lord. In verses 29–31 comes the heart of

Paul's faith about how to live in the world: "let even those who have wives be as though they had none....For the present form of this world is passing away." We know from what Paul has already said that he does not mean to abstain from normal married relations. In all these patterns of social existence (he goes on to list several) one is to live "as if not." The structure, whether marriage or some other pattern, is still there and has to be recognized; but it does not supply the energy with which the life of faith is lived. It is no longer important in comparison with the new world of faith and community that has opened up and that will, so Paul believed, soon come to be the only reality.

Paul believed that faith offered the possibility of living with marriage, with grief at loss or joy at the unexpected gifts of life, with dealings with money, or with engaging in the "world" in general, without being bound to these relationships. His "as if not" expresses a freedom to be engaged in all these things without being attached to them, which is more important for understanding what he was saying in chapter 7 than are the details about marriage patterns. This is the "eschatological freedom" which sprang from, and was Paul's interpretation of, his faith that the end was near, and that what had been begun in Christ would soon come to its fulfillment. How to find such freedom today, when the apocalyptic hope in which Paul found this freedom is no longer a viable possibility for most Christians, is a central question in interpreting this chapter. We shall try to deal with it in discussing chapter 15.

The transition from this fundamental statement of faith back to the specific problems of marriage comes about with Paul's remark that his aim is to free them from anxiety (verses 32–35). The point is clear that marriage, with its anxiety to please the spouse, may divert one from Christ. The language is unclear at one point, whether "anxiety to please the Lord" is good or bad. It is usually taken to be a good anxiety, but Paul may be understood to hope that faith will lead to a responsiveness to God that is even free of this anxiety. In other situations, of course, Paul included anxieties among the hardships that fall to his lot as apostle (2 Corinthians 11:21b–12:10; cf. 1 Corinthians 4:9–13, where "anxieties" are, however, not explicit).

7:36–38 Engaged Couples

Finally Paul returns to the question of the last major class of persons discussed. This section, therefore, can well be regarded

1 CORINTHIANS

as the concluding part of the preceding one. The discussion returns to the "virgins" (verse 25; who reappear in verses 36–38 in the NRSV as the "fiancée"). The obscurity of this translation reflects the vagueness of our knowledge of just what situation Paul was addressing. Here, too, in contrast to most of the chapter, Paul did not try to balance the responsibilities of men and women; the man decides about the marriage of his "fiancée." Though some scholars thought that Paul was speaking of the father's decision about his daughter's marriage, it is almost certain that the man who decides is the fiancé. The unease with which some couples were approaching marriage reflects the same question about sex with which the chapter opens. It has even been proposed that already in Corinth there were couples who had taken permanent vows of a chaste life together (so NEB: "if a man has a partner in celibacy," verse 36). This custom is known from later in the life of the church. This is not impossible; the engagement without marriage that is the other alternative is not too far from such a practice anyway, in terms of its personal meaning. However, the advice that Paul gives is basically the same as what has come before. If the man needs to marry, it is all right, but it is even better not to. It is often said that Paul "implies" that the woman is to share in the decision. But the traditional male-oriented pattern asserts itself here in that Paul does not sense the need to raise this question.

7:39–40 A Brief Comment About Widows

The discussion of marriage closes with a brief note about widows. They had already been included in "the unmarried and the widows" of verses 8–9; this passage is not different except for its repetition of the requirement that a woman is not free to remarry so long as her husband is alive. But, when widowed, Paul closes this long discussion, "in my judgment she is more blessed if she remains as she is. And I think that I too have the Spirit of God" (verse 40).

Preaching and Teaching on
1 Corinthians 7

Paul's specific guidelines for marriage were basically three: (1) marriage is thoroughly acceptable within the Christian community, though for those who do not need to marry, the way to

74

wholehearted service to Christ will be found by remaining unmarried; (2) the decision to marry, however, is an irrevocable
one, canceled only by the death of one of the partners. The need
for pastoral flexibility in applying this guideline is shown by
the exceptional case in which a nonbelieving spouse may ter-
minate the marriage. Paul also conceded that separations might
take place. And he specifically avoided advocating the principle of only one marriage per lifetime; (3) within this set of
rules Paul went far (but not all the way) toward advocating a
mutual equality of men and women within marriage.

If one considers these points in the context of the digressions of the chapter, several themes can be seen that are important for the modern interpreter.

The first point is not one articulated by Paul, but it is an
important one for us as we think about the meaning of the
chapter. Paul's obvious confidence that a definite profile of
marriage could be established within the church was related
to a feature in the life of the church that is not characteristic of
most modern Christian communities. So definite and distinct
a pattern of marriage cannot be maintained except in a separated community; one could say, in a sectarian community. A
strong commitment to permanent marriage cannot be maintained as a separate item of belief or practice, but it can exist
only where a strong sense of "apartness" and community life
exists, and where members of the group mutually reinforce,
with positive and negative sanctions, the common standard of
marriage. The early Christian community was, to a large degree, such a group. Most churches today are not. Paul did not
speak of this aspect of the marriage of members of the church,
though he did speak of the separateness of the Christian community in other regards (e.g., 6:1–11, on lawsuits). As we saw
in discussing chapter 6, Paul's vision of a separate community
was also far more open than first appears—a fact that produced
much of the tension that runs through 1 Corinthians. For the
most part he assumed that the new vision of faith established
a boundary that maintained the distinctiveness of the community, even as its members engaged in many sorts of social relations with outsiders.

In our own interpretation of the connection between what
Paul says about marriage and the traditional Christian teaching about marriage generally, we need to reflect about the community base that supports, or does not support, a particular

vision of how men and women relate to each other in marriage. Christian groups that interpenetrate the general society as thoroughly as most churches do today will inevitably find the standards of the wider society impinging on the marriage patterns of their members. To recognize this honestly is essential to discovering ways in which we can help people to relate to the New Testament views of marriage. We can best do this not by insisting legalistically on specific patterns, but by discerning directions of movement in the New Testament writings.

What is most distinctive about the Pauline message as a whole is not its ethical standards, but its faith that ethical failures can be and are forgiven. Both in continuing marriages and in the lives of persons whose marriages do not continue, all too often Christian evaluation has been far too judgmental. It is our faith that new beginnings can be made, even though we carry large traces from our past with us. From Paul's time to today, the possibility of using the faith in forgiveness as an escape from responsibility has been a possibility. But that possibility must not hinder us from proclaiming and counseling in terms of new beginnings and full forgiveness of past failures. That will mean taking account of the past and dealing with it, but not being bound by it. "You were bought with a price; do not become slaves of human masters" (verse 23).

Another aspect of the claim for permanent marriage was something about which Paul did speak very clearly. The new view of marriage that Paul offered was part of a vision of life transfigured by the powers of the new age. Paul could speak of marriage without making the exceptions and allowances that are required in an imperfect world, because he saw marriage in the context of a new world, a radical transformation of life. Perhaps to our surprise, the new vision sharply relativized marriage, made it less important. Paul made marriage meaningful by making it only a small part of life.

Marriage is being relativized in very different ways in our society, and, as noted at the beginning of this chapter, the immediate reaction of the Christian interpreter of life is usually to try to counteract this relativizing by stressing how important marriage is. It is worth asking whether the modern interpreter would not do better to follow Paul's lead, and try to deepen the meaning of marriage by relativizing it, by showing that it is not the center of life. In particular, if marriage can be seen in another framework than the quest for personal fulfillment, if it can be a part of a larger vision of giving oneself to life, it may attract the kind of lasting commitment that Paul presupposed.

We may call attention to the discussion of teenage sexuality and spirituality in the book *Now What's a Christian to Do?* edited by David P. Polk, for an approach to some of these issues from the contemporary side.

At the same time, this comment exposes one of the factors that is absent in Paul's words about marriage—the sense of venture. We may assume that Paul did not regard the "covenant" of marriage as merely a legalistic agreement ("covenant" is not a New Testament term for marriage, but it conveys the sense of commitment that Paul presupposed). But in chapter 7 he showed no interest in the life of marriage as risk and venture, as "story." Life was full of risk, venture, and story for Paul, but he focused on the gospel and on the life of the community, not on the life of the married couple, as the locus of this encompassing and risky venture. He attempted to "neutralize" the claims of marriage in order to free up this other, for him far more important, arena of encounter between God and human beings.

We may safely venture a comment, though Paul did not discuss the question, about why there is no reference to love between the partners in a marriage, in Paul's discussion of the subject. He does presuppose mutual concern and mutual responsibility, and much of what he says about marriage is cast in terms of equality, of give-and-take, of a small and definite circle of responsibilities. Some of what he says, however, is one-sided and patriarchal. Love as Paul will present it in chapter 13 is unbalanced, not concerned with give-and-take or equality. It was common to speak of love in marriage in Paul's time as in ours. If we are a bit put off by Paul's not doing so, we may well be stimulated to ask whether we do not too easily confuse various meanings of love. Surely there is room in marriage for the spontaneous generosity of which Paul will speak in chapter 13. But marriages are not built solely on this nor do they endure on it. They endure, as Paul rightly saw, on some form of mutuality. How to understand and speak of the interplay and relationship of give-and-take and equality on the one hand, and sheer spontaneous generosity on the other, is not a simple task. It is one of the challenges that the chapter leaves with us precisely by the fact that Paul was wise enough not to offer an oversimplified or romantic solution to this question.

To say this is not to downplay the important and continuing, indeed basic, contribution of spontaneous generosity in lasting marriages.

Finally, chapter 7 is as revealing as any other part of the letter on the question of how life may be radically transformed. Both Paul and his audience believed that faith in Christ brought about a radical transformation of life. But in contrast to many of them, Paul insisted that the transformation now known was only a foretaste of what was to come. Thus he did not expect the social structure within which the believer lived to be changed. At this point the preacher or teacher will have to ask how the gospel's claim on believers differs today, when we stand at a distance from Paul's urgent eschatological hope. We must consider the ways in which change in the inherited structures may be an appropriate response to the gospel in our situation, in cases where this question was not important for, or not faced by, Paul.

In particular, the transformation of patterns of marriage toward a full equality of men and women is a major task for today, and one that Paul did not anticipate. Here many of the women at Corinth had a deeper understanding than he did.

What most deeply animated Paul on this point was his conviction that one could not improve one's fundamental position before God by improving one's status in these social structures. That does not mean that the transformation of faith was purely inward, however. On the contrary, faith generated a new responsiveness to God and a new community that was to be the new center of concern. Not only so, but in spite of Paul's emphasis on remaining in the state in which one was called, in practice the new faith did open the way for some transformations of the social pattern—in the present case particularly in the greater equality of men and women in marriage.

For the modern reader, the question to be faced about the transformation of which Paul wrote is not so much whether we can relate it to specific questions like marriage just as Paul did. Rather, we should ask what equivalent there is today for the urgent conviction that it is close to the end of time. This conviction furnished the structure for Paul's liberating faith in the transformation of life. We shall return to this question in the discussion of chapter 15.

8:1—11:1 Love and Knowledge in Conflict Over the Question of Food Sacrificed to Idols

The Structure of the Passage

The next main question is how to deal with food sacrificed to idols (specifically, it is a question of meat), but his response to this question takes Paul far from the specific issue to reflect about consideration for others in the church and the tension between such loving consideration and self-assertion. The interweaving of themes sometimes makes it difficult to follow the connections among the various issues that Paul presents. The question itself was probably suggested by the Corinthian letter just as the question of marriage had been. (The clue is the phrase in 8:1, "Now concerning..."; this probably refers back to their letter; compare 7:1, 25). In Paul's (Jewish) background, if not in the background of many of his audience, the worship of idols and wrong sexual behavior were closely linked; see, for instance, Numbers 25:1–9; Exodus 32:6; Hosea. Thus this new topic follows naturally from the preceding discussion of sexual questions, and there is a unity to the whole of 1 Corinthians from 5:1 to 11:1 that might easily escape a modern reader.

The section is a complex one because it interweaves several themes. Its overall plan is the familiar A, B, A' pattern: A: 8:1–13, on love, freedom, and knowledge as shown in eating food sacrificed to pagan gods; B: 9:1–27, on the consideration (love, though he does not call it that) that Paul showed in renouncing his right as apostle to be supported by the church (this, too, is a question of food); and A': 10:1—11:1, once again on the question of food sacrificed to pagan gods, though this time the question is first approached indirectly, by making a distinction between two kinds of eating. Two illustrations of the dangers of idolatry precede the return to the main theme. First (10:1–13) is a typological interpretation of the Israelite wandering in the desert, to warn against falling into idolatry as many of the Israelites did (and eating was one feature of their idolatry). (A typological interpretation is one that sees the Hebrew Scripture as presenting a type or pattern of what was to be more fully seen in Christ.)

Then (in 10:14–21) comes a contrast between eating the Lord's Supper and participating in pagan sacrifices. These two paragraphs warn against actual participation in the worship of other gods. They are followed (10:23—11:1) by a return to the original theme of consideration for others rather than the exercise of one's isolated freedom. Thus there is a tension in what we have called A' (10:1—11:1). The last main portion of this discussion (10:23—11:1) comes back to the freedom to eat food sacrificed to idols, since it is mere food consumed by the body of the person who eats it, as in A. But the first two portions of A' bring in a different factor, making the point that eating in shared religious-social occasions (sacrificial meals) may release a destructive demonic power, since such social meals vitally participate in a forbidden pagan rite. In these two parts of A' (10:1–22), there is no question of love or freedom; this kind of participation is simply forbidden.

But in both A and A' the deeper point is that one needs to go beyond the rights and wrongs of eating food sacrificed to pagan gods and beyond one's individual freedom, by considering how one's action will affect others in the community. That is the deeper freedom.

That the B section in this structure (9:1–27) should illustrate the common theme (of consideration for others) with a subject matter very different from that of the A and A' sections is not surprising. We have already seen something similar in the way in which Paul inserted the question of lawsuits between two matters of sexual behavior (chapters 5 and 6), and smaller-scale examples of the A, B, A' pattern have also been seen before. Chapter 9 does complicate the overall pattern in a different way, because it brings up again the vexed question of Paul's authority and his sense of vocation. Though he begins by offering himself as an example of putting his rights aside, he is drawn into a passionate defense of his rights and authority as apostle. He is torn between presenting himself as an example of renouncing rights, and asserting his claim as an authority in the church. In this way chapter 9 "disturbs" the logical development of thought, just as has already happened when this same issue appeared in chapters 3 and 4. But as far as the structure of the whole section is concerned, chapter 9 belongs quite naturally where it appears, as a concrete example of the behavior that Paul is urging.

Thus the problem about the unity of 8:1—11:1 lies at a different point. In chapter 8 and in 10:14–22, food is neutral, once one recognizes that it is mere food. The issue is between this knowledge and the loving consideration of the other believer who has not yet come to understand meat in this way, and who thus fears contamination by the sacrificial rite through which the food has passed, even though she or he confesses the same Lord.

But in 10:14–22, prepared for by 10:1–13 and indirectly by 9:24–27, the point is that pagan liturgies do indeed transmit a sacred power, although it is a demonic one rather than a healing power. Paul warns against participating in the table of the Lord and also in the table of demons. In this perspective, food is not neutral. Both this line of thought and emphasis on the neutrality of mere food are deeply anchored in Paul's overall perspective, but one must reflect carefully to see how he could, so to speak, argue for both of them at the same time.

Thus these chapters form the strongest argument for those who say that Paul indeed wrote all of this section, but at two different times in two originally separate letters, with two different situations in mind. The 1 Corinthians we now read would thus be a composite letter made up from at least two originally separate letters.

This may be so, of course, but our recognition of the way in which Paul does not, as we put it above (pages 22–23) argue in a straight line, but rather presents his insights by moving around the topic, leads us to conclude that the passage is a whole. Despite its complexity, it was intended to have a fundamental unity. If the arguments do stand in some tension, that is best understood as a tension in Paul's own mind when he wrote. The discussion below will show how the parts are related. A point in favor of the unity of the whole section is that there is a substantial overlap of these same themes in Romans 14:1—15:33, where the same food question is followed by a discussion of Paul's own vocation. Romans was written from Corinth, and not long after 1 Corinthians. But the motif of the conflict between the Christian meal and the demonic presence in pagan sacrifices does not appear in Romans.

A further complication is that this whole discussion shows no awareness of the so-called "apostolic decree" of Acts 15:28–29, which lays down rules for non-Jews who become Christians, and which specifically forbids what Paul permits, that is, eating "what has been sacrificed to idols." Neither does Paul refer to this "apostolic decree," which forbids "fornication," in his discussion of intercourse with a prostitute in 6:12–20. Paul never appealed to this "decree," and as far as we can tell, neither did his correspondents in Corinth. According to Acts, the decision about the terms of non-Jewish entry into the Christian community had been reached in Paul's presence, prior to his arrival in Corinth. (The "decree" takes place in Acts 15; Paul arrives in Corinth in Acts 18.) Some scholars have suggested that Paul did not believe that the stipulations of Acts applied to Paul's predominantly Gentile congregations, but that is not the way in which Acts present the matter. It is more probable that Paul did not know about these minimal requirements for Gentiles, which may actually have been formulated at a later period.

We may come closer to understanding the way in which the parts of this section are related to one another if we turn from its specific content to notice the way in which its advice moves back and forth between speaking of a world in which the powers of evil have been neutralized (so that one is free to eat sacrificial food), and presenting a world in which threatening powers surround the believer, or are at work in his or her life (as in the contrast between the table of the Lord and the table of demons). When Paul writes directly of food offered to pagan gods, he thinks of a world in which the evil powers have been canceled, and the believer can (and must) exercise freedom. But this is not the whole story. From another point of view, the believer also exists in a still hostile world, threatened by demonic powers. This theme comes to the fore in 10:1–22, and the way for it is opened by Paul's presentation of his own struggle as he carried out his calling as apostle (in the latter part of chapter 9). The unifying thread of the whole section is the interplay between these two images of the world in which faith is exercised. Another way of putting it is this: when he thought of the Christian community as existing within secure boundaries, Paul spoke of freedom and love. But when he sensed that the boundaries were threatened and the identity of the group was being eroded, he drew on more conflictual images and insisted on sharpening the separation between those inside and the outsiders.

Thus the complex structure of this section, with its interweaving of themes that stand in great tension, is a reminder that for Paul love and freedom were not general principles that could be described systematically. Rather, love and freedom became real in concrete acts that took place in specific situations, and these situations both set limits and gave opportunities for freedom and love.

8:1–13 Love and Knowledge

As noted above, the question whether it was right to eat food offered to pagan gods probably came from the letter sent to Paul. Our letter also seems to quote other statements from the letter to Paul. (See the quotation marks in the NRSV.) Paul never does answer the question with a straight "yes" or "no," nor does he in fact say in so many words that he himself ate food that had been sacrificed to idols. We usually assume that he did exercise the freedom that he here defends (but cf. 8:13, where he mentions the possibility of giving up meat altogether). Instead of a yes-or-no answer, the whole section from 8:1 to 11:1 probes beneath the question to help Paul's readers understand the deeper issues that should influence a person's decision about the original question.

Before discussing the question at all, Paul looks at the stance of those who were claiming their freedom to eat. "All of us possess knowledge" (verse 1) makes sense as a statement from some of the congregation, not from Paul, since he later corrects it by saying that "It is not everyone…who has this knowledge" (verse 7). Though he will go on to agree with the content of the knowledge, he begins with a critique of this way of facing life. Knowledge, he says, "puffs up" in contrast to love, which "builds up" (8:1; cf. 10:23). The contrast between love and knowledge is a major theme of chapter 13, while Paul had confronted people whom he described as "puffed up" or "arrogant" (the same word in Greek) in 4:6, 19; 5:2. Paul could speak of "knowledge" positively (1:5), but here it is a risky possession, akin to the "wisdom" that he had criticized in chapters 2 and 3. There wisdom was contrasted with the cross; here knowledge is set over against love. Knowledge closes one off from community; it is isolating and self-deceptive, because it tends to make one aware only of one's own situation. Love, on the other hand, "builds up," a term that Paul regularly uses for the growth of community, of shared life.

Somewhat surprisingly, Paul speaks of the love that stands over against knowledge as loving *God* (verse 3), rather than of the human love that builds community, which we would expect from "love builds up" (verse 1) and as we find love described in chapter 13—but this is explained by the primary focus of knowledge as *knowledge* of God, which is "reversed" in love by the believer's being known by God, that is, acknowledged by God. Paul did not mean, however, that by love one earns God's approval, but rather that love manifests that God knows a person.

Paul next agrees with his questioners that an "idol" has no existence since there is only one God, and likewise only one Christ (verse 6). This confessional statement, which may be in part at least already traditional, in turn was a modification of the Jewish confession of the one God. God and Christ are coordinated as the ones on whom we depend—all comes to be "from" God the Father, and "through" Christ. Paul assumes that Christ was a pre-existent power, the one "Lord" coordinate with the one God. This confessional statement is fully in harmony with belief that Christ had accompanied the Hebrews in the desert, in the typological interpretation of Scripture in 10:4.

Note, however, that this monotheistic confession is, if not qualified, at least complicated by the recognition that in some sense there are many "gods" and "lords" for others (verse 5), though not for us. This statement moves away from a theoretical discussion about God to a recognition that people are powerfully shaped by what they believe in. Even "we" who confess the one God and one Christ have to take account of the seeming reality of these many "gods" and "lords" as we deal with those to whom they seem real. This point opens the way for the discussion of how to get along *within* the community when there are different opinions about the dynamic powers of life.

As he often does, Paul lays a considerable groundwork before he states his main point. The nonexistence of other gods means that food sacrificed to them has not been harmed, so that we are free to eat it. So far Paul agrees with what his correspondents seem to have said. But, in contrast to the claim of 8:1 that "all of us possess knowledge," here Paul makes the point that not all do have such knowledge. Some would eat this food as if it were tainted by the sacrificial process through which it had passed. Thus "your" freedom may lead a "weak" believer (or a person with a weak conscience [verse 7]) into real trouble—such a person may actually be "destroyed" (verse 11) by your knowledge. It is important to see that the whole passage is addressed to the "strong," though Paul does not use that term here (cf. Romans 15:1). The "weak" are not addressed by Paul.

In this chapter, in contrast to chapter 10, the power of pagan gods and of the food dedicated to them is purely an imputed power. It is because people think that there is power in them that they affect both pagan believers and "weak" Christians. The confession of the one God and one Christ cancels this power to those whose vision is fully transformed by faith. Paul definitely includes himself in this group. It is noted that to "others" there are many gods and lords, but not to "us." Yet it turns out that "we" are far from being a homogeneous group. We, monotheists though we are, also include those for whom pagan gods still exercise a defiling power.

Paul is not in the least concerned about what the actual worshipers of pagan gods think about Christian dietary practices. This question simply does not come up. But the mixed character of the Christian community does require that the knowledge of the "strong" not be the only guide to behavior. Knowledge tends to separate. Paul is not thinking of the separation between believers and nonbelievers. That was a "good" separation, as he has said in chapter 5. Insofar as the knowledge that there are no other gods separates a believer from a pagan, that is all to the good. But despite the seeming definiteness of the line of separation, there is a confusing overlap. Some are not yet ready to exercise their freedom, for the mysterious power of the sacred food still affects them. They are, nevertheless, fellow believers, and their situation is as important for "me" or for a "strong" believer as is my own. So Paul urges that if it is harmful to one of the "weak," then refrain. He closes with the probably exaggerated rhetorical statement that he himself would give up meat altogether, if his eating it would cause a fellow believer to stumble.

The striking phrase "those weak believers for whom Christ died" (verse 11) is a reminder that in the face of the graciousness of God in Christ, the distinction between the weak and the strong is erased.

The vision of chapter 8, then, is a vision of a community in which the right to exercise power is freely waived in favor of a considerate love for others who are different from oneself. The nonexistence of other gods frees "us" from the threat of their power, but that does not free us to exercise our own power, but rather to be open to others who may be different from ourselves, and to consider how they may be affected by what we do.

What can we know about the two groups, those who "have knowledge," and those who do not, and about the power struggle between them that Paul tries to modify by writing this chapter? Interpreters tend to go in one of two directions: either those who claimed knowledge were "gnostics," with a special religious and theological point of view that emphasized freedom, especially freedom from physical things, or they were the well-to-do, who could afford meat, while the weak were the poorer members of the community who seldom ate meat in any case, and to whom it therefore would more easily retain its strangeness if it had passed through a sacrificial procedure.

Difficult as it is to establish the picture of economic conditions at Corinth, there was no doubt a strong economic element in this debate. Most people in Corinth ate meat infrequently, many of them hardly ever. It was only the well-to-do for whom the question of food sacrificed to pagan gods was a frequent and recurring one. At the same time, the very possibility that the "weak" could be tempted to eat this meat is an indication that meat was not excluded from their diet.

This chapter leaves us with a sense of unfinished business. The ethical point is clear: what links me to my fellow believers is more important than my individual freedom. But the context is not clear: what is the setting, the flow of powers, in which we act? Paul's strong sense that the community was a focus for powers far more potent than the individual's choice of whether to eat meat will come up again in chapter 10 (and with a different emphasis, in chapter 11).

9:1–27 Paul's Own Practice as an Example of Setting One's Own Claims Aside

As we turn from chapter 8 to chapter 9, our first impression is of an abrupt change of subject. Not only does the focus shift from sacrificial food to Paul's claims as apostle, but the theme of a challenge to Paul's authority comes in again. This theme had already thrust itself into chapters 1—4, and there, as here, it makes clear how complex is the interplay between strength of self and the setting aside of the claims of the self. Paul sets out to show how he has put his claims aside, just as he is urging those who find that they are free to eat food sacrificed to idols to set their claims aside. But as he uses himself as an example, he finds that he has to defend and justify his position of authority. As the chapter develops, it focuses more and more sharply on Paul's own vocation and on his struggle to be fully committed to his calling. Yet chapter 9 does give a very direct comment on the theme of the previous chapter, which is taken up again in chapter 10. Paul had not claimed his right to support as an apostle; if the readers are to imitate Paul (11:1), they will likewise be willing to give up their right to eat meat that had been sacrificed to pagan gods. This is the theme that links the chapters together. It is the fundamental point that Paul is scoring even though he comes at it indirectly, and does not reach it in this chapter until verse 12b.

It is also true that as he reflects on his apostleship, other questions come up besides the motif of setting one's rights aside. The special difficulty is that to Paul himself, he was a clear case of putting his rights aside for the sake of the gospel, but there were those who thought that his consideration showed that he was weak or even that he was not really an apostle. Much of what Paul says is directed against this challenge. Thus the chapter holds two conflicting motifs in tension.

Most of the commentaries pay scant attention to the way in which the question of food links chapters 8 and 9. It seems to the scholars that food offered to idols is so different from food given to support an apostle or missionary that the food question is only incidental. If we remember, however, that food (meat) offered to pagan gods was real food—in fact, was the highly desirable yet scarce protein—we can see that in both cases the issues are not disembodied theological questions, but were matters of physical support and sustenance, not to say survival. Different as the questions are, they are linked by the way in which both of them bring together a basic question of physical existence with a faith that claims that physical survival is not the most important thing. Both chapters advocate putting food (=survival) in a larger framework in which the structure of human caring, grounded in the gospel, controls how one nourishes oneself and survives.

In the long section 9:1–18, Paul's status as apostle gets much more space than his renunciation of the rights of an apostle, but both themes are fundamental. He cannot let go of the defense of his rights, once he has claimed them, but returns again and again to this theme. This is a sure sign that this was a controversial issue. He could not simply note that though he was an apostle, he had not claimed the "food and drink" (verse 4) that were his due. For it could appear, and apparently did appear to some of the Corinthians, that Paul had held back from claiming his rights because he was not secure in them, since he was not really an apostle, or was one only marginally.

What Paul meant by "apostle" was a person called by Christ to share in the completion of Christ's work. (See above, pp. 42–45). An apostle was called by the risen Lord (verse 1, "Have I not seen Jesus our Lord?"; cf. 1 Corinthians 15:8; Galatians 1:15–16). But not all who had seen the risen Lord became apostles (not all, for instance, of the "five hundred" of 1 Corinthians 15:6). On the other hand, neither did Paul restrict the group of apostles to "the twelve plus himself," as some Christian writers did later on. Here, for instance, Barnabas is included among the apostles (verse 6). It is evident that who was an apostle was a debatable question, and we do not know enough say exactly who were apostles in Paul's opinion, nor to fill in the picture of what view of apostles was held by those in Corinth who raised questions about Paul.

What makes it difficult for Paul was that his vocation included a powerful inner certainty, a certainty that defined for him who he was—yet this certainty could never be fully shared with other people. It was always possible to dispute it. So Paul appeals to the pragmatic evidence—you, the church in Corinth, are the proof that I really am an apostle, at least to you. This last concession (verse 2) is tantalizing, for there is no way to know whom Paul had in mind as those to whom he was not, or could be thought of as not, an apostle. In the flow of his discourse, that is not really an important question. He is stressing the point that those in Corinth, at any rate, are evidence that he is an apostle.

This tension between inner certainty and practical proof runs throughout the history of Christianity. In Paul's time there was no established hierarchy to determine who could be a church leader. As the church developed, one of the main reasons for the growth of church authorities, typically bishops, was to determine who could be accepted as a leader. Many of the groups that resisted the developing organization of the church did so in order to claim a greater degree of spontaneous freedom for those who believed that they were called to positions of leadership in the church. As far as the specific "office" of apostle goes, however, it dropped out in almost every form of Christian church. The apostle was too closely linked with the very beginning of the church in the resurrection for this type of leader to continue into later generations.

What comes to the fore in verses 1–18, however, is not the general question of whether Paul was a real apostle, but the more specific question of what it means that he has failed to claim his right to support. A word of caution is in order here. We do not know the details of his means of support. He claims that he met his daily needs by working for a living (9:6; cf. 1 Thessalonians 2:9), but he may also have received gifts from some of the congregation, stayed in the homes of leading members, or, perhaps, had part or all of his fare paid when he sailed across the Aegean Sea. Though he speaks in broad terms, he is not necessarily claiming total financial independence from the Corinthians (though he comes very close to this in 2 Corinthians 11:7–9). What he does claim is that he basically maintained himself instead of accepting daily support from the community.

What is striking is that Paul exerts so much effort to prove that apostles generally have the right to be supported by the church. First comes the example of "the other apostles and the brothers of the Lord and Cephas" (verse 4), an example which is all the more interesting because it includes also the right to "be accompanied by a believing wife" (verse 5; "wife" is surely the right translation, as against "woman," i.e., woman servant, though we may assume that often, in accord with the customs of that time, the wives of the apostles did indeed "serve" them as they traveled with them).

Then comes the commonsense argument, the argument from "human authority" (verse 8): ordinary workers, such as soldiers, vineyard workers, or shepherds, receive wages in money or in kind. Next Paul turns to the revealed will of God, the law of Moses. The ox is not to be muzzled as it is treading out (threshing) the grain (Deuteronomy 25:4), and this command becomes a figure first for the farmer who directs the ox, and then by a further derivation, for the apostle who, carrying forward the farming metaphor, has sowed "spiritual good" and may rightly "reap...material benefits" (verse 11). This image links the passage to 3:5–9, where "planting" and "watering" were images of Paul's and Apollos' work.

Most interesting is the way in which, as Paul reads the Law, the literal meaning is swallowed up in the interpretation. Jewish interpreters also understood the Deuteronomy passage to say something about the farmer's rights, arguing from the "less" (the ox) to the "greater" (the human being). But they also retained the original meaning; the ox is indeed not to be muzzled.

Paul does not quite say that God does not care for oxen, but he comes very close indeed to this as he throws out the rhetorical question, "Is it for oxen that God is concerned?" (verse 9b; the Greek form of the question expects the answer, "No!"), thus canceling out the literal meaning of the passage in favor of the allegory that he reads out of it.

We may regard this scriptural interpretation as one sign of a shift from an agricultural to an urban setting for Christianity, a shift that in time separated the church from an awareness of our connection with the life-giving powers of the earth and led to the supposition that God is indeed not concerned for the earth or the animals, but only for human beings. Paul did not go that far, but his urban background gave him little sensitivity to the earth. This incidental reference points to a process that we are only now beginning to understand and to reverse.

Noting that unlike others, he has not exercised this right, Paul continues with his illustration of how deeply rooted in reality the right is, now with an illustration familiar both to Jews and to non-Jews from the income of priests and others who serve temples; they share in the offerings. A final, clinching argument is that "the Lord commanded that those who proclaim the gospel should get their living by the gospel" (verse 14; cf. Luke 10:7–8; Matthew 10:10).

This is a curious argument. Why did Paul labor so hard to prove that apostles, including himself, had the right to support when, as he says repeatedly, he did not want to claim this right? The point is clear if indirect: only if the right is admitted can Paul speak from a position of strength. The argument is not really about whether apostles had the right to be supported by the churches, despite the fact that is the way in which Paul casts it. What is really at stake is whether Paul belongs to the group who have this right. At this early date there were no hard-and-fast definitions of who was and was not entitled to support by the local congregation—either in the church at large or in Corinth. Paul's not accepting support could seem like weakness, as if he did not really belong to the inner group of leaders. In a different connection this same issue appears in 1 Corinthians 15:8–11, where Paul boldly lists himself with the other apostles and even claims to have done more than they have.

Verses 15–18 make clear the thrust of what has come before. All the arguments about how right it is for those who proclaim the gospel to live by the gospel have not really been directed toward establishing a general principle (for the principle seems to have been agreed upon by all concerned; see verse 12). Rather, the elaborate justification of the custom is precisely the basis for Paul's rejecting it, or more correctly, going beyond it. His calling asks him that he not merely proclaim the gospel, but that he make it "free of charge" (verse 18) to highlight its nature as gift.

This short section beautifully illustrates the interlocking relationship between Paul's vocation to social transformation and his own struggle with his vocation. The whole section, 8:1—11:1, deals with a community problem, and chapter 9 is brought in to illustrate how to deal with a question in interpersonal relations. Yet as he sets forth his role as apostle, Paul turns from the social relations side of it (his right to be supported, on the one side, and the goal of salvation, on the other), to a concern with his own status, to his "ground for boasting" (verse 15). It is no wonder that Augustine and Luther read Paul with so strong an emphasis on the inward side of his faith. Even though interpreters today rightly turn away from this subjective side of Paul, we can see that the structure of these chapters, with this reflection about his own status at their center, shows that Augustine's interpretation was in touch with a real element in Paul's writings.

"Boasting" has already been a theme (see above, pp. 32–33). Here Paul paradoxically claims a ground for boasting in the very course of an argument that he does not have any claims, and is only fulfilling an obligation that has been laid on him. "My reward is to take no reward" (Wetstein, *Novum Testamentum Graecum*, II, 136) tells part of the truth, but only part. For the deeper paradox brings Paul back into the social world: he claims a role of leadership that is based on his being a vehicle rather than a self-asserting person. The tensions in this model did not originate with Paul. It can already be seen, for instance, in the Hebrew prophets. And these tensions are still with us today. Do we want a leader who is wholly self-effacing? What of the danger that such a man or woman will introject his or her own need for status into the vocation?

These issues are the more important since they are not directly in the focus, but show themselves as Paul struggles to affirm his right even though he has not claimed it.

Paul's practice is illustrated in the next paragraph (verses 19–23). He has been glad to adopt the different lifestyles of dif-

ferent kinds of people, and that means setting his own prefer-
ences aside, in order to make the gospel available to human
beings in their manifold differences. In making the point he uses
bold rhetoric—speaking of himself as "outside the law" (verse
21) in his dealings with those who are themselves outside of
the law, and saying that he became "all things to all people"
(verse 22). It is noteworthy that he here includes the "weak,"
among whom he became weak (verse 22), since they have been
the subject of chapter 8. Since it is "all for the sake of the gospel" (verse 23), we glimpse the deeper factor that gives coherence to this otherwise pragmatic, almost opportunistic-sound-
ing behavior. This paragraph is a fine commentary on chapter
8, since it shows the background for the kind of consideration
that Paul there advocates. Consideration for the brother or sister is the other side of the coin of "for the sake of the gospel."
The two cannot be pulled apart.

The last statement of the paragraph leads to the next (verses
24–27), with its surprising shift from the gospel as being something for others to being something for Paul himself. No doubt
the point of Paul's bringing in his own struggle to remain faithful to the truth that had laid hold of him was intended as a
rebuke to those who thought that any such struggle lay behind
them.

10:1–13 The Threat of Idolatry: An Example from the Past

There is an abrupt change of subject with 10:1–13, though
as one reads on, connections with what comes before and what
will follow become clear. Paul draws a parallel to the current
life of the community by calling on them to remember the experience of the Israelites in the Exodus and the wanderings in
the desert. Though apparently few of the Corinthian Christians
were Jews, Paul takes for granted that all of them live out of the
memory offered by the Hebrew Scriptures (some later gnostics
would deny this).

The stories of the Exodus and the period of testing in the
desert provide warning examples to the church at Corinth. Thus,
though the subject matter is entirely different, the theme of the
danger of not remaining faithful links this interpretation of scripture to Paul's account of his own struggle to remain faithful,
which has just preceded it (9:24–27).

This striking way of reading the scripture was a traditional
one. This passage may well have been formulated by Paul be-

fore he wrote the letter, but apart from that, he draws on a long tradition of looking at the desert period as a time of testing and temptation. The list of Israelite failures, drawn mainly from the book of Numbers, was developed from the text of the Hebrew Scriptures and not from the specific situation at Corinth, as is shown by the way in which the errors are drawn so narrowly from the text of the Hebrew Scriptures.

The tradition of remembering the period of wanderings in the desert as a time of testing was already part of the text of Exodus and Numbers, and it was further developed in Jewish reading of the Scriptures. Paul follows tradition in reading the Bible from the vantage point of the present situation. The warning element in those ancient experiences applied both the original Israelites and also to "us," "on whom the ends of the ages have come" (10:11). The parallels that Paul sees between "then" and "now" make it appropriate to speak of this as a "typological" interpretation, that is, an interpretation in which a pattern of experience in the ancient text foreshadows a later experience in the life of the community of faith. Later on, this kind of interpretation was highly developed, but it would be a mistake to think that Paul was looking for a rigorous pattern of correspondences or "types" between the Israelite and the Corinthian experiences. He read the biblical story as a warning.

The scripture is here linked to the present, of course, by the list of Israelite mistakes that serve as moral warnings to the church at Corinth (10:6–10, drawn particularly from Numbers 11:4, 34; Exodus 32:4, 6; Numbers 25:1–18; 21:5, 6; 16:41, 49). But more fundamentally, the parallel is founded on the similarity of the crossing of the Red Sea to Christian baptism, and of the eating and drinking of the Israelites to the Christian Lord's Supper. They were "baptized" into Moses in the cloud and the sea, and they ate and drank the "spiritual" food and drink that God provided (10:1–5). It would be wrong to ask how narrowly Paul drew the parallel between the present sacraments and the Israelite practice. Viewed from the perspective of the present, Paul can see that "the same thing" was going on in the earlier period.

The point of the parallel is clear. "All" (repeated for emphasis in 10:1, 2, 3, 4) the Israelites received the great gifts and privileges. But "most" of them did not respond rightly, and God was not pleased with them (verse 5). Paul believed that there were those at Corinth who were in danger of taking for granted their security in faith, and he uses the Israelite story with telling effect to warn them. They will be sadly deceived if they think that merely participating in the rites of the church will keep them clear from the danger of the failure of faith and the dangers of the surrounding world.

In this setting, eating and drinking at a sacred meal have become powerful carriers of a sacred power. Though eating and drinking do not guarantee security, they are sacred acts, in sharp contrast to the neutral food of chapter 8. In this situation the presence and the power of the one God and the one Christ do not neutralize the power of other gods, but rather serve to create a community that is different from the surrounding world, and that must maintain its distinctiveness. Therefore they call for a response that separates the believer from the world.

The image of a "real presence," a real divine presence with the Israelites, is already clearly in the text of the scripture, in the "pillar of cloud by day...and...a pillar of fire by night" (Exodus 13:21; Paul refers only to the cloud). Also the desert situation implies that eating and drinking are not to be taken for granted, but are special gifts of God—the manna and the water that springs from the rock. Jewish interpretation had drawn all these images into a unity by saying that God accompanied the Israelites in the form of the Wisdom of God, which was the "flinty rock" from which the water sprang when they needed it (as in the Jewish philosopher Philo, *Allegories of the Laws*, 2.86). Paul reshapes this reading of the text by seeing all these manifestations of the divine presence, already in the days of Moses, as the presence of Christ: "...the rock was Christ" (10:4). Christ was the presence through which God was with human beings and with the world from ancient times, indeed from the beginning. This scriptural interpretation is an application of the same confession as in 8:6, "...one Lord, Jesus Christ, through whom are all things and through whom we exist." It is coherent with the "logos" or "Word" Christology of the early church, even though the "logos" terminology does not come from Paul but from John 1:1.

But Paul was not interested in developing his beliefs about Christ. That was left for later writers. We see a beginning of this development in Colossians 1:15–20 and Ephesians 1:15–23, both of which probably do not come from Paul, but from a slightly later time. Here in 1 Corinthians Paul is scoring a basically ethical point: the presence of Christ in our sacraments today does not set us free from the need for serious ethical struggle and decision, but rather puts us in the position where we can truly make the right ethical decisions. The monotheistic background of the whole discussion is, in a very traditional way, the background for a decision "against the world."

Thus the section ends, just as had chapter 9, with a call not be to "cocksure" (Conzelmann, *First Corinthians*, 168), not to take for granted that Christ has given us a position of security. The Corinthians are told to expect troubles. It would be wrong to try to distinguish sharply between the meaning of "trials" and the meaning of "temptations" for the word translated "testing" in 10:13. Both inner temptations and outer trials are included. Such troubles are the normal human lot, but God will see that the believer is not tempted or tested beyond his or her capacity. Thus it is up to the Corinthians to stand firm.

There are times, alas, when this statement of Paul simply is not true. Many are tested beyond their capacity, and are broken by the experience. It would be a narrow and mean reading of Paul to blame such persons as if "it was their fault" for not being open to the divine assistance that was available. Paul writes from the vision of a time of trouble that the believing community will have to endure, and out of the faith that God will not abandon them in such a time. In other words, he was writing to men and women who were, he believed, living in the "last time" (cf. 7:25–31). He calls for more than resignation and endurance in the time of trouble. You, he held, as believers, are called to take part in the struggle of the last times. His own vocation as apostle was also part of this struggle. He did not stop to work out the interplay between this faith that the community would survive, and the harsh fact that individuals may not. Thus, though we must reject an individualistic and moralistic reading of these verses, we may find in them great encouragement and moral resource for living in the "last times" that we ourselves face.

10:14–22 Participation in the Lord's Supper

A second illustration of the way in which our life is not built up just by individual choices, but also by pervasive powers that surround us and are within us, is provided by the Lord's Supper. The Supper is a "sharing" (verse 16) or participation in the blood and the body of Christ. The Lord's Supper appears again in 11:17–34, where the emphasis will be on its power as a reenactment of what Christ has done for us. Here the emphasis is on the actual presence of the Lord as we take part in the Supper.

In a distinctive and powerful way, this meal brings the community into the field of force that is Christ. Paul is not concerned to describe how this takes place; rather, his point is the contrast between the "field of force" of Christ and that of the competing, destructive powers. Much scholarly ink has been spilled over the question of how much of the background of this meal was Jewish, and how much Greek. Interpreters have often assumed that "Jewish background is good, Greek is bad," moving from these very chapters with their sense that the pagan liturgies were the bearers of demonic powers. But the distinction between Jewish and Greek or pagan contributions to Christian practices and beliefs is a false one. Paul and other early Christians were profoundly influenced by both, and these two "backgrounds" deeply influenced each other.

Distinctively Jewish practices, such as the blessing of the cup at the close of a meal, and the sense of participation in God's presence in the sacrifices, surely contributed to the Christian Lord's Supper. But a theme that was shared with "pagan" religions also contributed: the sense that a liturgical meal was a sharing in the presence of the deity. Indeed, Paul's whole discussion would lose its force unless he was speaking from a recognition of this similarity.

The listing of the cup first, and then the bread (verse 16) does not describe an actual liturgical practice. (The order, bread first, then the cup, appears in 11:23–26). Rather, the bread is put last to link the end of verse 16 to the following statement, that those who take part are *one* in partaking of the one bread. It is unwise to probe Paul for an answer to the question, "Just how is the Lord present?" Centuries of theological discussion have been devoted to this issue, usually making distinctions that had not occurred to Paul. We may at least say that for Paul, Christ was present not so much specifically in the bread and wine as in the whole shared action.

Three points are brought to the fore in this brief reference to the Lord's Supper. First, it serves to bring people together ("we who are many are one body, for we all partake of the one bread," verse 17); this is reinforced by referring to the way in which, in the Jewish sacrifices, people are brought together as they become "partners in the altar" (verse 18). Second, the power of this sharing of God's presence is somehow similar (though with an opposite value) to the sharing in a rite of another faith. Paul does not seem to believe that the sacrifices of other religions had a power to create community, as the Lord's Supper did, but these sacrifices were nonetheless vehicles of power—negative power. This is the point of the second half of the paragraph: the sacrifices to "idols" are not to a god, but they *are* rituals that recognize and release powers that are greater than human: the power of demons (verses 19–22). The third point is that if these two fields of power are mixed, that is, if people take part in both, they will be "provoking the Lord to jealousy" (verse 22). It has often been noticed that the imagery of the "cup of demons" (10:21) stands in tension with the assertion of 8:4 that "no idol in the world really exists." We do well to acknowledge the tension. It is a recognition of the vitality, albeit, Paul thinks, a destructive vitality, of other faiths. Hence he holds that, instead of taking part in a constructive, community-building field of force, those who try to participate in both areas will be threatened by the destructive power of the very force that creates community.

We shall have to reflect about these three points below, in the section on preaching and teaching on this passage.

10:23—11:1 Freedom and Consideration Once Again

The concluding paragraph of this long and complex section returns to the starting point: the freedom to eat is strongly affirmed, but it is juxtaposed to the freedom to be considerate of someone with different convictions. The return or recapitulation is sharply marked by the quotation of a Corinthian slogan from an earlier section: "all things are lawful" (verse 23; cf. 6:12), which is parallel to the "all of us possess knowledge" of 8:1. Once again Paul speaks from a position of confidence in the inner coherence and vital strength of the community, from a position of confidence in the strength of its boundaries. Thus the issue of conflicting kinds of worship (10:1–22) is set aside. "The earth and its fullness are the Lord's" (verse 26, from Psalm 24:1) again expresses the faith that the opposing powers have been canceled. The freedom that results is spelled out in detail. On the one hand, in the market you are free to buy meat without asking whether it has passed through a sacrificial rite. And you are also free to accept an invitation to dinner from a nonbe-

97

liever. Such dinners were sometimes held in temples, and Paul does not rule out this possibility. The passing note that Christians might dine socially with nonbelievers is a most revealing glimpse into the social life of the Corinthian Christians. Paul did not expect that the strong sense of a separate, coherent life of faith would exclude such social contacts and the friendships that they presuppose. As we noted above, Paul's openness was possible because of his conviction that the Christians were already definitely separated from nonbelievers. At the same time, we have seen in the immediately preceding section that Paul recognized that the power of faith to maintain the distinctiveness of the Christian life required the setting of limits. Here he believes that he can leave such limits aside.

Here, in other words, despite the setting of meat purchased where pagans would also purchase it (thus giving up the necessity for any special rules about Christian food), and even more so, despite the setting of a meal hosted by a nonbelieving friend, Paul's attention is focused on the internal relations of the community with itself, on, as he says, things that "build up" (verse 23; compare the use of this term in 14:4, 17, and already in 8:1). The maxim in verse 24, that you are to seek not your own good, but that of your neighbor, governs the whole section. As the whole development in chapters 8 through 10 has shown, in this discussion Paul has in mind primarily the fellow believer as the neighbor.

At the same time, the concluding advice, to "give no offense to Jews or to Greeks, or to the church of God, just as I try to please everyone in everything..." (verses 32–33a), is a reminder not only of the importance of deepening our interrelatedness, but of how complicated it is to do so—for Paul's pleasing of everyone was anything but a meek giving in to what others in the church preferred.

Preaching and Teaching on 1 Corinthians 8:1—11:1

The pervasive theme of this section is love as consideration for a person whose judgments are different from your own. It is a theme that runs through much of the letter. In addition to what is said above about this theme, let us note two points.

First, Paul is at his best when he argues for understanding and consideration of a kind of person whom he has himself tried to understand. The "weak" of chapter 8 are a case in point. He specifically notes that he had tried to empathize with them (9:22), and as a result this whole discussion of how to respond to them has depth and flexibility.

When Paul had not been able to enter imaginatively into a stance that was different from his own, he was much less successful at applying the principle of consideration. His affirmation of women was partially successful, partially a failure (chapter 7; see on 11:2–16 below). Thus the challenge of moving from the text to our own situation does not lie simply in applying Paul's specific advice. It is a question of entering into the process of understanding, of which he gives such powerful examples, and in going beyond his specific example when it is appropriate to do so. Standing at a distance from him, we can see that we are called upon to expand our openness to the "otherness of the other" in ways that Paul might have been unable to do.

A second comment is that this whole section is a fine example of the tension between setting one's own claims or views aside and affirming oneself as a person of dignity. Paul is so well worth getting to know because he struggled with this tension so deeply. Surely it appeared to many of those who encountered him that he was simply self-assertive. That may in fact have been how his influence worked in many specific cases, and that stance was an element in his practice—as appears in some of the recent books written about Paul by scholars who are women. (See especially Elizabeth Castelli, *Imitating Paul: A Discourse of Power.*) Rather than thinking of Paul as a monolithic thinker, however, it is more adequate to see his thought and imagination as woven out of various strands. The strand of imitating Paul as conformity to the single standard that Paul sets is certainly there, but it is woven into a complex texture in which the importance of an open community having real variety in it is just as central if not more so. Thus the call to imitate Paul, as he does Christ (11:1, at the very conclusion of this whole section) is the climax of a section that calls for variety in the community. If we look at Paul's struggle with himself as he discloses it in his letters, we are brought into the presence of a classic and profound case of a person with a powerful sense of vocation who is trying to be self-critical as well as self-expressive—a stance well illustrated by the contrast between the openness of 9:19–23 and the determined dedication of 9:24–27. This aspect of chapter 9, along with other things that Paul says about himself in this letter, will interact profoundly with our own learning about how to stand up for our convictions in a world where convictions all too easily lead to polarization. For Paul, the figure of Christ provided the focus that held in creative tension the two aspects of commitment: involvement in and wholehearted dedication to a cause, and openness to change in how one understands and acts for the cause.

In the background of this lengthy section lies another fruitful tension: the tension between an open community and a community that is sharply set off from the rest of the world. The community of believers is radically open—it makes a place for all sorts of people, and they are not expected to become alike. That point is illustrated here by the tension between those who find it acceptable to eat food sacrificed to idols and those who do not, but that is only an illustration of the endless differences that appear in any open community. It is central to the whole of 1 Corinthians that there will be great variety in the church, that it will be truly open.

On the other hand, the community will be bound together by a common commitment and a common impetus or lure toward transformation—Christ or the Spirit. For Paul this means that the church will be sharply separated from the "world." Yet the boundaries are in many ways "porous"—as in Paul's openness not merely to food sacrificed to idols, but perhaps even more significantly, his openness to friendships and meals with nonbelievers. It would be a bad misreading of this openness to think that it existed simply for the sake of persuading people to become Christians. Surely that was important, but the common humanity of those within and outside the community, their common reach toward life, is the deeper foundation.

In our time we hear calls for renewing and accentuating the separation between the church and the world, which is one side of the picture sketched above. All too easily such calls tend to cancel out the variety of the community that is equally central in this letter. A central task in bringing the insights of 1 Corinthians to bear on our life today lies in rediscovering the interaction between commitment and openness. Too often the reading of Paul listens only to the side of his thought that emphasizes boundaries. An attentive listening to this section of the letter can open us to a deeper reading, which will lead us toward rethinking what an open community can be.

Another aspect of openness also calls for reflection. For Paul it was impossible to "partake of the table of the Lord and the table of demons" (10:21). Here community (the sharing of the bread and wine) is not simply the personal interaction of people who held a variety of convictions, but a shared act that is a special vehicle of power. The sacred rite of dedicating meat to another god was neutralized by the knowledge, shared of course with the Jewish tradition, but for Paul given through Christ, that such gods were not actual. But the same was not the case for the sacred meal. Both the Christian meal and the non-Christian one were carriers of power in a special way, and to try to mix these powers could only be destructive.

We shall return to the question of special power in cultic acts when we reflect about 11:17–34, where Paul again deals with the Lord's Supper. For the present passage (10:14–22), the point to consider is the contrast between Paul's conviction that to mix these two kinds of participation was destructive, and the openness many Christians adopt today toward taking part in, say, a Hindu or Buddhist rite if they are invited to do so. What makes the difference?

We may sort out four possible ways of understanding this change. A first way would be to regard such a shift in Christian practice as itself destructive, and to reassert the exclusive practice that was obviously right to Paul. One has to respect this effort to continue unchanged in the inherited patterns of the faith, but this option will not commend itself to those whose actual experience of other faiths has shown them that these other paths are to be respected as genuine channels of helpful religious power.

A second path would be simply the conviction that the sense of holiness, of the immediate presence of a mysterious power in the ceremony, that Paul took for granted, has been lost, and cannot be a part of contemporary faith, which must be a matter of personal conviction rather than of cultic practice. Ours is a time when many have lost the sense of awe that Paul expressed; it is a secular time. Such a view can be connected to our text by expanding the neutralizing power faith in Christ, that here applies only to the dedication of meat to an "idol," to neutralize also such rites as sacred meals. Such a move would probably also make the Lord's Supper much less awesome than it was to

1 CORINTHIANS

Paul, as it indeed has become to many even very devoted Christian worshipers today.

We believe that a deeper encounter with the text will move away from either of these ways of viewing it, to reconsider the way in which God's power is at work in the world. Paul recognized a role in creation for Christ: "Jesus Christ, through whom are all things" (8:6), though his very strong focus was on the death and resurrection as disclosing the meaning of Christ.

One may move toward a greater openness to other faiths by expanding the role of Christ in creation, looking in all faiths for elements that they share with faith in Christ. This is the third option of the four listed above. This path has the strength that it connects with many studies of early Christianity that show how much the new faith adopted from its environment, both Jewish and "Greek." From this point of view one might respond to an invitation to take part in a ceremony of another faith—as a respectful outsider, of course, not as a believer in the other faith—with a sensitive openness to what one found that connected with what one already had experienced in Christian faith.

A fourth possibility is not entirely different from the third, but it sees the meeting of faiths differently. Recognizing that one may find something like what one has already come to know, one might respond to the invitation mentioned above, not so much in the expectation of finding what was already known, but rather in the hope that a creative enlargement of one's own faith might take place, precisely by finding something different. This way of reappraising Paul's strong condemnation of sharing in rites of other faiths would ground itself in the character of the transformation that Christ works, a transformation that opens one to truth and to a wider reality. There is much in 1 Corinthians that would support such an effort to hold in creative tension the gifts that one had already received in faith, with new and perhaps very different insights. It would not be necessary to suppose that the Spirit of Christ was the source of all the new that one came to bring into one's vision, but Christ would be seen as the lure to creative transformation that makes the expansion of vision possible.

11:2—14:40 SECOND MAIN SECTION OF "SPECIFIC ISSUES":

Issues in the Conduct of Worship

The long section, 5:1—11:1, has been concerned with a range of issues that we might call interpersonal morality, mostly questions of sex and idolatry. For Paul, individual and social aspects of human behavior were so deeply interconnected that it would have been impossible for him to separate individual ethics from social ethics, as many do today. The discussion above of the issues in chapters 5—10 has shown how thoroughly interpersonal and social Paul's reflection about questions of personal behavior was.

The next major section, 11:2—14:40, deals with issues in the conduct of worship. Naturally the social aspect of behavior comes very much to the fore, but the same interplay between the individual's responsible decision and the web of relationships that makes the decision possible is evident in his comments on the questions about worship. In dealing with a variety of issues, he repeatedly warns against expressing one's freedom in a way that ignores the context and the relationships that make freedom possible—the same pattern that he had used in dealing with the questions of "ethical" conduct in the preceding section.

As we shall see, much of the tension in these chapters arises from the conflict between Paul's conviction that to respond to the context means to fit into an orderly pattern of expectation and his openness to the new. He anticipates that many of his hearers will be more ready to scrap these conventional expectations than he thinks is right. Here we come upon a contemporary question for the churches. Paul's issues were different from ours: appearing and taking part in worship in a "get up" expressive of one's sex; sobriety at the Lord's Supper; orderliness in the spontaneous contributions to worship. But the question of how far one needs to be "conventional," that is, to act in a role established by the society, in order to be responsible to the context and to the web of relationships that make one's existence possible, is a very lively one in the churches today. What seemed like chaos to Paul may well have seemed like creative spontaneity to many of those to whom he wrote. Thus, this section is exceptionally rich in provoking thought about flexibility and change *versus* conventional expectation in our own situation.

The section can be outlined as follows:

11:2—14:40 The Conduct of Worship
11:2–16 The Proper Appearance of Women (and Men) in Worship
11:17–34 Danger in the Lord's Supper
12:1–31a Tests for the Suitability and Value of Gifts of the Spirit
[12:31b—13:13 Love as the Highest Gift]
14:1–40 Suitable Ways of Speaking in Tongues and Prophesying

11:2–16 The Proper Appearance of Women (and Men) Who Speak in Worship

This is a very obscure part of the letter. The main point is clear: Paul strongly believes that women who speak in worship (pray or prophesy) are to present themselves in a conventional form of appearance. It is not clear just what details of their clothing or hairstyle Paul was thinking of, and the theological reasons that support his view are very difficult to understand. It is clear that Paul expected resistance to what he was asking.

On first reading the introduction to the passage is a surprise. Paul praises the Corinthians highly for following the traditions that he had brought them (11:2), but then very abruptly begins to argue against an unconventional appearance of women who speak in worship. We may assume that Paul expected that women who did not actually speak would also follow the custom he advocated. Perhaps the shift in tone that follows verse 2 shows that the tradition he had taught (and for which he praises them) included the practice of women speaking in worship, but these words of praise may be more general. He does offer his view on the appearance of women as a new teaching, however; they had not heard it from him before. (On the question of women speaking in worship, see also 14:33b–36, where women are forbidden to speak in worship.)

Though Paul introduces his theological explanation first (11:3), let us consider the practice in question. It is evident that Paul believed that women should look like women, indeed, like proper women. Traditionally this has been taken to mean that a woman should wear a veil in public worship (11:5–6). On this interpretation, Paul was pressing the Corinthian women to adopt a Jewish practice, for the wearing of veils in public by women seems to have been customary in Jewish communities. It is not known exactly what the custom of Greek women in Corinth was.

However, there is no word that clearly means "veil" or "veiled" in the whole passage, despite the way in which this term appears in almost all translations. The Greek terms mean "covered" or "a cover."

Though the church soon interpreted Paul's words as meaning that a woman should wear a veil at worship (and later, a covering of some kind on her head), in its original setting Paul's strong advice may have dealt simply with hairstyles. He speaks about how long hair is appropriate to a woman (11:15); he scornfully remarks that if a woman will not cover her head, she might as well have her hair cut short or shaved close (11:6); and he specifically speaks of her hair as a "covering" (11:15; not the same term in Greek, however, as used before for "uncovered").

Thus some interpreters think that it was a question of keeping one's hair properly dressed, in a traditional coiffure, instead of letting it hang loose, as women did in some of the other religions of the time, especially in ecstatic worship, and that the question of a veil does not come up at all.

In either case, we can see the influence on Paul of what we may call "middle class" standards of proper behavior. Whether it was a veil or a way of wearing the hair, neither the very poor nor the very rich would have felt the same need for conformity that Paul did.

We should add that Paul balances his advice to women with the corresponding pattern for men: they should wear their hair short, and (if veils come into the picture) not be veiled (11:4, 7). It seems likely that the advice to men comes in to reinforce the "equality and justice" of proper behavior; both women and men have a proper standard. However, it is unlikely that men in the church in Corinth were wearing their hair long.

Now, Paul's reasons. First he sketches a "wisdom" argument, reasoning from God's creation of men and women. God is the *head* of Christ, Christ the head of man, and man the head of woman (11:4). "Head" probably means both "authority" and "source." Paul draws on Genesis 1:26 for the dependence of human beings on God as their "head," though of course the term *head* does not appear there; and on Genesis 2:21–23 for the belief that woman is derived from, and therefore has a *head* in, man (cf. 11:8). As he restates his theology of creation, he uses more biblical language: man is the image and reflection of God; woman is the reflection of man (11:7). His formula allows that woman as well as man is made in the image of God; he does not say that woman is the image of man.

The word translated "reflection" above (from the NRSV) is literally "glory." It seems that in Paul's thinking God's glory is passed down the series of beings: Christ, man, woman—each successive stage having less glory. Nevertheless, the woman's presence is potent with power to disrupt the harmonious flow of power in worship. It is important for her to function only in her appropriate place.

Just why this is so important is far from clear. A woman of inappropriate appearance would offend God and shame herself. Somehow, too, she would be upsetting to the angels (11:10)—though this verse brings in another puzzle, the "authority" on the woman's head. This can mean either that the woman has authority to decide about her appearance, and is really responsible for it (the more normal way of taking the term "authority"), or that she is subjected to the authority on her head. If one accepts the series of stages as really indicating that women are farther from God, it is easy to conclude that they ought to stay in their appointed place.

But this whole picture is offset by the equality of men and women "in the Lord," which stands in great tension with everything that Paul maintains. Neither one is independent of the other; woman came from man (in creation), but (in the normal course of birth) man comes from woman (11:11–12). Since woman also comes from woman in this same way, this balance is not quite as equal as Paul makes it. But it does assert an equality that stands in real tension with the whole course of Paul's theological or "wisdom" argument. Also striking is the way in which Paul draws on the natural process of birth to show how something is true "in the Lord."

Perhaps because he recognizes the tension between his reasons for understanding how men and women are related in the Lord and the two distinctive forms of appearance that seemed so important to him, Paul turns to a different argument, the argument from "nature." "Does not nature itself teach you that if a man wears long hair, it is degrading to him, but if a woman has long hair, it is her glory?" (11:14–15a). Finally he appeals to custom, his own ("we have no such custom") and that of the churches of God (11:16).

We do not know as much as we would need to know about the customs of women's appearance, whether in dress or hairstyle, to judge very clearly how far the women Paul criticized were "shocking" conventional people in the congregation. Their style may have been well accepted by the church, or there may have been some protests. Living as we do in a time of very flexible styles of clothing and hair, it is hard for us to understand why the question was such an issue. It seems to have been important to some of the women to have the freedom to express themselves in prayer and prophecy by adopting a special appearance.

One may conclude that the wisdom argument is not very good theology, because it is at odds with the equality of men and women "in the Lord," and that it would have been better simply to appeal to "nature" or the common sense of the time— even though we know today that nature has very little to do with these matters. Those who defend this piece of Paul's theology do so on the ground that the outer structures of life are not transformed by faith, as Paul himself partly holds in chapter 7. The problem with this is that his interpretation makes no place for change, although the gospel was a potent force for change. So a more considered reaction is that it is important to try to draw lines between one's theology and concrete issues like this. If the result is as unfortunate as it is here, that requires us to start over and make a better theological interpretation. This case well illustrates the two-way flow between theology and practical issues. The attempt to move only in one direction, from theology to the concrete problem, can easily bring unten-

1 CORINTHIANS

able results as it did here. A final comment is that it is very clear that Paul had not tried to enter imaginatively into the position of the women in question, as he had tried with the "weak" (8:7–13; 9:22).

11:17–34 Danger in the Lord's Supper

The previous section began rather surprisingly with a commendation (11:2). In contrast, this remarkable discussion of the Lord's Supper begins with "I do not commend you" because of a way of celebrating the Supper that is not only wrong but dangerous (11:17; cf. verse 22).

Though many details are obscure, the general picture is clear. Paul has learned that what should be a solemn entry into and participation in the presence of Christ has become an ordinary clique-centered supper. As a friendly group gathers, they eat together with what they have brought, not thinking of the latecomers who may be able to bring little or nothing.

We do not know how accurately Paul was informed about the Corinthian practices. He does not say where he learned about their conduct. Nor do we know whether there was a disagreement within the community about the manner in which the Supper was being celebrated. We usually assume that there were good grounds for Paul's rebuke.

Clearly the Lord's Supper was a real meal, at some point in which, probably at the end, the sacramental action was celebrated. But it cannot really be celebrated if the congregation is broken into groups that ignore one another's presence. Paul used the same phrase, "divisions among you" (11:18), that he had used at the very beginning of the letter about the factions who appealed to different founding figures (1:10), but he probably does not mean that the divisions or factions at the Lord's Supper were the same as those that claimed Apollos, Cephas, Paul, or Christ as their heads in 1:10–17. We do not know whether there was any significant overlap between the two sets of "factions."

We do know from records of other sorts of fellowship groups that existed at the time that shared meals where everyone ate their food together were familiar, as were meals where smaller groups had their own separate dishes. It seems likely that the differences that Paul found wrong were largely economic. Those with more means and leisure came early and settled down to their own better meal, perhaps in the dining room, while those of more modest means, probably coming straight from work, ate what little they brought separately, perhaps in the court-yard that was a feature of most substantial houses. (See Charles H. Talbert, *Reading Corinthians*, 75). Paul assumes that the whole congregation gathered as one for the celebration—but he says that in fact they were not one in the way in which they came together.

So the central thrust of his admonition is an ethical one: if you ignore your connection with people who are different from you, you cannot be open to the power that flows from the sacrament, or this power will become destructive to the community.

Paul does not just give ethical advice. He has a practical solution: if you are hungry, eat at home first (11:22, 34). Just how much of a meal would be left to share in common is not made clear. Paul's suggestion may have been a first step toward transforming the Lord's Supper, over the course of time, into a token, symbolic meal instead of the real meal it evidently still was in the Corinth of Paul's time.

As so often in 1 Corinthians, Paul's ethical advice is joined to a powerful sense that as we come together, we are not only in the presence of and responsible for one another, but also in the presence of and responsible toward a mysterious, dynamic presence that may be destructive as well as healing. He connects what he has heard to be disorderly conduct at the Lord's Supper with the misfortunes that have fallen on some in the community. "For this reason many of you are weak and ill, and some have died" (verse 30). Though his positive advice is naturally focused on the individual who must see whether she or he is fit to take part in the meal, Paul does not say that those who became ill or died were the same as those who misused the supper. No, the destructive power acts on the community as a whole.

To correct the situation, however, Paul's advice is naturally more individualistic: "Examine yourselves, and only then eat of the bread and drink of the cup. For all who eat and drink without discerning the body, eat and drink judgment against themselves" (11:28–29). To discern or recognize the body means both that they be aware that the Supper gives the body of Christ, and that the body of Christ is the group of believers.

Nevertheless, God's judgment on those who believe is remedial rather than destructive; "we are disciplined so that we may not be condemned along with the world" (verse 32b). This conviction has already appeared in earlier references to the judgment of believers (3:15; 5:5).

It is in this setting that Paul recalls the tradition that he had received about the Supper, a tradition that came "from the Lord," though he does not mean that he received it directly from the Lord; Paul had received it from others who were in the church before him (11:23–25; verse 26 is probably Paul's addition to the tradition that he had received). The tradition is not brought in to guarantee the historical accuracy of what is said or done in the liturgy, but to show how such potent power comes to be there. The Lord's Supper is a reenactment or re-presentation of the action by which Jesus offered his body and blood and identified these with the nourishment of the Supper.

Modern readers are naturally interested in comparing this account of Jesus' Last Supper with those in Matthew, Mark, and Luke (which, of course, had not yet been written). That is an important question, and Paul's words are the earliest record we have of the Last Supper. But they are not a historical record in the narrow sense. Paul's account is a "foundational story," a story that gives the basis for one of the basic practices of the Christian group. As such it has been shaped by the meaning which believers found in Jesus and in the Lord's Supper as much as it has been shaped by memories of Jesus' last days. So the meaning of the crucifixion, which is so closely linked to the Lord's Supper, is known in the experience of the community and expressed in this solemn account.

As Paul saw it, the Lord's Supper looked both to the past and to the future. "Do this in remembrance of me" (verses 24, 25) is more literally translated, "Do this as a memorial of me" (NEB). The more literal translation rightly puts the emphasis on the liturgical act rather than on the memories of the worshipers. Some interpreters think that the "memorial" is meant in the sense of a "reminder"; the Supper is a way of reminding God of the promises made in Christ. There is good precedent in the Hebrew Scriptures for calling on God to remember the promises. But it is more natural to take the "memorial" as a solemn reminder to those who take part, of the basis of their faith.

In concluding Paul adds a note that points to the future: "you proclaim the Lord's death until [the Lord] comes" (verse

26). This note of hope and anticipation pervades the Supper, as well as the backward look. As the congregation celebrates, it looks forward to the "more," to the fulfillment that is yet to come. Though Paul does not mention the resurrection of Jesus in connection with the Lord's Supper, the forward look of hope (which becomes the focus in chapter 15) is part of their faith because Christ is known daily as a transforming presence.

Preaching and Teaching on 1 Corinthians 11

The central ethical point of both parts of chapter 11 is the same: act with consideration for those who are different from you. This has also been the ethical theme of the preceding section, chapters 8—10, so that this theme links these parts of the letter. As we saw above, this is central and very important advice, one of the enduring legacies of 1 Corinthians. Though this theme is not explicit in 11:2–16, where women are urged to follow a conventional pattern of appearance, this consideration for others is a basic reason why, in Paul's opinion, it is important for them to do so. That is clear from the fact that it is public gatherings that are in question.

Similarly in 11:17–34, where a careless and dangerous way of coming together for the Lord's Supper is the issue, it is precisely the way in which they, or some of them, ignored others who were different that is the heart of the issue.

Thus, what was said about chapters 8—10 applies here as well. A community in which very different kinds of people can be truly open to one another is at the heart of Paul's vision of what Christ brings about. It is worth repeated efforts to understand and to appropriate into our own situation.

At the same time, just as we saw in interpreting chapters 8—10, more needs to be said. The open community can only be a mutual community. If there are two sides, both sides need to reach out toward each other. There is a place for patience, and for adjusting (as in the case of the public appearance of the women) to conventional, probably rather middle-class standards. But there is also a place for challenging the conventional ways. There has to be a place for that move of challenge in the open community, or it will stagnate. If we knew better what the customs of the time were, and what the exact proposal was that

Paul made, we might well be more positive than he was toward the women who asserted their place by an unconventional
appearance. It would be narrow and unwise to believe that it is
only by giving in to the sensitivities of the "weak" or conventional that the true community is formed. If Paul's emphasis on
harmony sometimes gives this impression, we must remember
that his words were only part of a dialogue, in which he was
learning as well as teaching. The limited nature of this section
is clear enough from the way in which nearly all churches have
abandoned the long-standing practice of asking women to cover
their heads in church.

It would be hard to make a similar case for the clique-centered celebration of the Lord's Supper.

Especially in reading the section on the Lord's Supper (but
the same question can be raised less directly about the previous
section), a modern reader must ask about the potent sense of
divine power in the liturgical act, which was so obvious to Paul.
When Paul is in conflict with the Corinthians about their words,
about what they say, he counters with the same medium—his
own words. But when it is a case of an inappropriate liturgical
act, he believes that God will act directly and negatively. Hence
the threat in 10:22: "Or are we provoking the Lord to jealousy?"
and the conviction that sickness and death are sent by God in
response to the wrong celebration of the Lord's Supper (11:30–
32). Again, when God's destructive judgment has to be released
in punishment, this has to be done in a special liturgical act
(chapter 5).

Later discussion of the Lord's Supper has concentrated on
the tension between seeing that it has power because it is a form
of proclamation ("you proclaim the Lord's death..." [11:26]),
on the one hand, and seeing its power in the mysterious presence in the bread and wine ("this is my body..." [11:24]), on the
other. For understanding 1 Corinthians, it is important to ask a
more general question: can we enter into the potent sense of
divine power in a liturgical act that Paul presupposed? It is too
simple to contrast "magical" rites, which are believed to bring
about their effect simply by correct performance, and rites that
express faith, which are powerful only when faith responds to
them. Put this way, Paul certainly believed that faith was necessary for right or real performance. But we need to take account of the way in which, for him, the Lord's Supper had holy
power even when entered into wrongly.

If we presuppose that it is only in the Christian "sacraments" (however many they may be) that the mysterious power is present, we miss the broader sense of liturgical power that we find in Paul. His conviction that pagan sacrifices also carried special power, and his belief that the Christian rite could be destructive as well as healing, were also part of his understanding of mysterious power.

The question is important because we live in a time in which the power of the holy has largely receded from consciousness. (See also the discussion above, on 10:14–22.) In the Introduction we mentioned that the New Age movements of our time could be helpful in understanding Paul's conversation partners—precisely because in the varied New Age groups we see a partly "premodern" but also a partly "postmodern" sensitivity to a mystery that pervades life. At the point of cultic ceremony, these New Age movements can also help us understand Paul. They remind us that life is shot through with mystery, and that this mystery is a potent force. Uneven as they are in depth of insight, they can remind us of the more-than-rational awareness of the holy presence of God with which Paul approached the liturgical acts not only of his own faith but of others as well. Further, the fact that people turn to these groups is a reminder that the acts that focus on the mysterious presence of God or Christ are not fixed. Symbols may lose their power, as Paul Tillich reminded us. We believe that our Christian symbols and rites are capable of renewal, and that they can speak more profoundly to us than many of the practices on which New Age groups focus. Nevertheless, Christian symbols do not exist in a privileged space that separates them totally from others, and we can learn a great deal from the openness to mystery in such groups. That does not mean being uncritical of them, especially of their frequent separation between spirit and body, and their usual concentration on the individual's state rather than on interactive, social living, in both of which traits they are probably similar to some of those in Corinth. (For a sympathetic Christian appraisal of New Age movements, see Bruce G. Epperly, *At the Edges of Life: A Holistic Vision of the Human Adventure*.)

These New Age movements are sharply set apart from Paul by the way in which, for him, a valid expression of God's mystery comes only through Christ. We have presented above, in discussing the possibility of taking part in a ceremony of another faith (pp. 102–104), several different ways in which such a larger view of God's presence can be related to Paul's Christ-centered one. These options also apply here.

12:1–31a Diversity of Gifts and One Spirit

The "gifts" of chapter 12 are not all exercised in worship, so this section well illustrates the interplay between worship and the rest of life. Yet the chapter leads up to chapter 14, which is sharply focused on worship, and many of the gifts discussed here are expressed in worship, so the theme of the community at worship continues in chapter 12.

The plan of the chapter is the familiar one, A, B, A'. After a brief but very important introduction (verses 1–3), the discussion of the diversity of gifts is divided into three parts: A (verses 4–11) on the variety of gifts given by the one Spirit; B (verses 12–26) on the various parts of the body harmoniously contributing to one another, as an image of the harmonious variety in the community; and A' (verses 27–31), again on the variety of gifts.

12:1–3 Testing the Spirits

The setting of worship is presupposed in verses 1–3, which offer a test for the authentic presence of the Spirit: "...no one can say 'Jesus is Lord' except by the Holy Spirit" (verse 3b). This confession is contrasted to what Paul assumed was the empty inspiration offered by other gods (verse 2), and to the enigmatic cry, "Let Jesus be cursed" (verse 3a). This phrase may have been invented by Paul as the opposite of the true confession, or there may have been circumstances, no longer clear to us, when it was actually uttered. The confession of Jesus as Lord presupposes that the Spirit is a new power that comes into a person, or, we may perhaps better say, a "field of force" into which a person enters. It is usually assumed that "Jesus is Lord" was an ecstatic cry, spoken when a worshiper was carried away, but this may not always have been the case.

Paul well knew that people not only were constituted by their culture and their past as well as by their own choices, but that they also entered into new "fields of force" that brought new possibiilites into their lives. His point is that Christ is the criterion for judging the truth, the correspondence to reality, of any such new transforming power. In our final section, we shall think further about this test of transforming powers.

12:4–11 Different Gifts

There must be some consensus within a community about the powers at work in it; otherwise it would not be a community. That is one side of Paul's identification of creative power with Christ—the continuing activity of a definite presence, shaped by the story of Christ, makes the community the "body of Christ" (verse 27) so that it has a coherence and consistency that make it distinctive, different from other communities.

But his emphasis throughout the chapter is on another point: this is the kind of power that makes for variety; it is expressed in many ways. This point is introduced, at the beginning of section A, by the threefold formula: varieties of gifts from the "same Spirit," varieties of services, but the "same Lord," varieties of activities, activated by the "same God" (verses 4–6). This "trinitarian" grouping of Spirit, Lord, and God is a spontaneous formulation, rather than the expression of a dogmatic tradition. There is no thought that the three figures do different things; rather the point is that they jointly produce different activities that mutually work for the common good (verse 7).

Then follows a list of gifts (verses 8–11), gifts that range from wisdom and knowledge (it would be foolish to try to distinguish these), "faith" (here similar to the faith of 13:2, a special faith that produces unusual results), gifts of healing and miracles, and then the gifts specifically expressed in worship: prophecy, discernment of spirits, and finally, "tongues" and interpretation of tongues. It is often said that Paul places these last two gifts at the end of his list, to remind his hearers that speaking in tongues was not as important as they thought. That may be true, but "wisdom" is the first gift here, though it was strongly downplayed in 1:18–25 and 2:1–5, so that it is wise not to lay too much emphasis on the rhetorical arrangement of the gifts. The main point is that all are real gifts, which are to be expressed in a harmony appropriate to their divine source. Here, too, a major point is that a person cannot choose which gifts come from the Spirit. It is the Spirit that chooses how they are distributed (verse 11). This is said to reinforce one of the major themes of the chapter, that all the varied gifts are from God, through the Spirit, and no one should consider himself or herself in a superior or elite class because of possessing a particular gift. The "anti-elitist" theme is one of the principal messages of 1 Corinthians as a whole.

12:12–26 The Body and Its Parts

Then Paul turns to the image of the body, which is one though it has many and varied parts (section B, verses 12–26). The solidarity of the community is driven home by two already-familiar illustrations of differences overcome: those between Jews and Greeks, and between slave and free (verse 13). It is often noticed that here a third pair is not mentioned: the one-ness of men and women, in contrast to Galatians 3:28, where all three pairs appear. (Compare 7:17–24, in a different context, for the pairs Jews/Greeks and slave/free.) Many interpreters hold that here Paul did not mention the third pair, men/women, because in this letter he wished to emphasize the subordinate position of women. That may be so; we have noticed in chapter 7 that the move toward full equality of men and women is only partly carried out, and we have seen Paul's convoluted reasoning about appropriate differences in the appearance of women and men in 11:2–16. But here it may be that two illustrations were felt to be enough.

Since in verse 13 we read both about baptism into one body and about drinking of one Spirit, some readers have concluded that the Spirit was first experienced when the new believer was baptized. But Paul does not say this. It is more probable that the first experience of the Spirit came before baptism, as a response to preaching, whether Paul's or someone else's.

With the image of the body, the function of worship slips into the background. The comparison of the church to a body brings together two different images: the church as the body of Christ (verses 12b, [13a], 27), and the more general image of individual persons as organic members of a larger "body," pictured after the need of the various parts of the human body for one another (verses 12a, 13–26). The image of the body and its parts was a common one at the time, and today as well it needs little interpretation. Sometimes the writers of the time used the body as a metaphor for the way in which the whole human community, or (as here) a particular human community, needs different functions, which must work together, while sometimes the image becomes a picture of humans in a much larger, cosmic society, of which humans are only a small part. This latter use of the image is far from Paul's thought. (See above on 9:9.)

The central thrust of the image of the human body is that human beings cannot be isolated individuals. In view of the place of the independent "self-made man" [sic!] in the mythology of our culture today, the reminder that different kinds of people need one another at a fundamental level is well worth emphasizing. Paul speaks directly to any individualistic piety of self-development with his familiar point that one part cannot be independent of the rest merely by saying that it is. Being together is a basic element of being at all. The point is most movingly expressed in the final sentence, that all the parts suffer and rejoice together.

Another aspect of the image is less often noticed. The need of the different parts of the body for one another presupposes that each person has a stable place. A body part cannot choose to be another part. This aspect of the image fits well with what Paul had said above in 7:17–24 about "remaining in the condition in which you were called." But remaining in one's previous condition may not have been what many of Paul's dialogue partners had in mind when they became Christians. A lack of a stable "social location," that is, of an established role in society, was probably characteristic of many new Corinthian Christians. They aspired to social mobility through their new faith. Here is a point at which we would do well to listen to the aspirations of those who did not wish to remain in the same social function. Paul may have pressed too hard for social stability at this point.

This becomes clearer if we note that the other image that is combined with the already-familiar image of the human body and its parts is by no means a stable image. The "body of Christ" (verses 12b, [13a], 27) is a dynamic image, an image of transformation. By sharing in the body of Christ, people entered into a new "field of force," as we said about the Spirit that is at work in the body of Christ. They cannot remain the same. They will act differently. First Corinthians allows us to see glimpses, for instance, of women who were standing forth and claiming new roles for themselves. Why should they not?

Many readers of Paul have tried to resolve the tension between stable social function (as wife, husband, slave, owner, etc.) and transformed action (as believer) by saying that the public, manifest side of the transformation was still to come, in the final resolution of the life of this world—but in the meantime one had to function within the already-established social forms. Paul partly believed this (perhaps too much), but at the same time he recognized that the transformation worked by the field of force of the Spirit of Christ refuses to be limited in such a way. Functions such as apostle, prophet, teacher, as well as speaking in tongues changed a person's social position even if they were not recognized roles in the surrounding society. We shall have to return to this question below.

12:27–31a Different Gifts Again

The final section of the chapter (A', verses 27–31) returns to the variety of gifts. Here we find a different list from that of verses 4–11, though both culminate in "tongues" and the interpretation of tongues. We would like to know more about just what the people did in the various categories. The list was probably put together from several already-traditional lists of functions. This is clearest with the first three: "first apostles, second prophets, third teachers" (verse 28); these were already established figures. We notice that Paul puts his own role, apostle, first. He probably did not originate this placement of his own role, and there is a tension between putting his role first (and speaking in tongues last, verses 28, 30), and his emphasis that no one is to claim a higher position than another. We have seen before, in discussing 4:1–21 and 9:1–27, that Paul's own claim to speak with authority can easily disturb the smooth development of his argument.

Two things are especially worth noting. First, under gifts of the Spirit Paul includes capacities that must have been evident before a person became a believer. Skill in "forms of leadership" (verse 28), for instance, may very well have increased markedly when a person was challenged by new tasks in the community, but to be a leader drew on capacities that the person brought to the life of faith. The point is that here Paul draws the life of creation into the work of the Spirit.

The second point to note is that the section ends with "But strive for the greater gifts" (verse 31a). This is in marked contrast to verse 11, where the particular gifts are chosen by the Spirit, so that no one should feel diminished because a more important gift had been given to someone else. But here the group is urged to aspire to and work for the "greater gifts." There is choice as well as simple receiving in relation to the gifts of the Spirit.

Preaching and Teaching on 1 Corinthians 12

Behind the specific gifts of the Spirit lies the conviction—shared by Paul and the congregation—that life is *open*, not simply determined by the past or by what we ourselves do and choose. We have used the term "field of force" to interpret the Spirit and the Christ (Paul uses both terms). Though the Spirit and Christ are sometimes spoken of as a field of force that determines the outcome, more deeply it is a liberating field of force that makes possible a fuller activity and a fuller mutual participation.

As modern people we understand ourselves as, on the one hand, largely determined by our past and our environment, yet, on the other hand, we claim at least a modest amount of freedom for ourselves. What Paul says about the Spirit cannot be exhausted by either of these ways of understanding ourselves.

The Spirit is an environment that, as the illustration of the body makes clear, opens us to an awareness of and a readiness for our connectedness, for dynamic interaction with other people (and, we may add, though Paul does not explore this point, with our whole environment as well). Living in dynamic interaction with others, in response to their presence, need, and stimulation, gives us a far richer freedom and humanness than simply living from our past and the present exercise of our individual freedom.

But the Spirit is yet more. We may call it a "lure," a leading toward transformation, toward new possibilities. The whole of 1 Corinthians is full of dialogue between Paul and the congregation about how to actualize the new possibilities with responsible care for the whole. And responsibility is central. But even more fundamental is the vision of life as lived in the environment of a liberating power that enables us to move beyond what is possible for us from the resources of our past and our present ability to manage ourselves. Here the faith both of Paul and of the congregation stands as a continual and fundamental challenge to the modern vision. It is both a theological challenge: how to think about the power that makes transformation possible; and a practical challenge: how to help our communities become places where women and men will become aware of this transforming power.

A second theme for interpretation is the relation between the Spirit and Christ. For both Paul and the Corinthians, the world was full of powers, of "spirits." Their world was not limited, as the modern world tends to be, to the past, the social environment, and the power of individual choice. Their problem was not whether there was a field of force beyond these factors, but how to distinguish among the various competing forces.

One test is the test of the felt intensity of the force. This test had great appeal to some of the Corinthians. Another is simply the mysteriousness, the "otherness," of the experienced force. We shall come back to these tests in discussing chapter 14.

For Paul there was what seemed to him to be a very definite test: only the Spirit of Christ is the Spirit from God, the Spirit that makes for wholeness and life (12:1–3). Paul does not use the phrase "Spirit of Christ" in 1 Corinthians, but Christ as the test of spirits is explicit through most of chapter 12.

This test seems clear enough, but it is not easy to apply it. "Christ" was for Paul precisely the transforming, unifying power at work in the church. "Christ" was an image, and like any image, was a woven texture of many elements. The Jesus known to the first disciples was one thread in the weave, but not a prominent one. Attitudes, visions, moral stances learned from other Christians, from Jews, from "Greeks," as well as Paul's and the congregation's continuing experience of God's presence in Christ all contributed to the image. "Christ" was (and is for all of us) a composite image, presenting to the imagination, to the choosing self, and to the group as a whole the transforming power of God. For Paul the image of Christ surely had a central strand—the cross. This again is a complex image, an image of the paradox of life through death, of finding through giving up. It has often been interpreted in a repressive or life-denying fashion, or in a manner that deprived the believer of responsibility—God has to do it all. (See above, pp. 40–42, on the cross.)

Thus, the Christ of whom Paul wrote was a flexible, growing image, as Christ has remained until today. It was precisely because the image of Christ could be transformed to include impulses from a wide variety of sources (at Corinth, for instance, the aspirations of women for a full recognition of their humanness and their ability to speak for Christ), that this image could and can remain vital. That means that today we cannot mechanically apply tests from the past or from, say, this letter, to decide whether an impulse is in touch with Christ. We have to discern the spirits with a sensitivity to what God is leading us to do in the present.

This point leads to a third theme for interpretation, a theme that is most obviously expressed by chapter 12. Cooperation, awareness both of the difference of the other and of the inexpressible value of the other, flexibility, readiness to listen, sensitivity to the hurt of the other as well as joy at the other's joy (12:26)—these marks of the Spirit of Christ are measures of real community, signs that people are open and ready to respond to one another. This is a wonderful vision, and one that calls for repeated renewal of our own vision of what community can be.

A caution is in order, however. All too often Christians have thought that such mutual openness could be realized in the unchanged present, a present time where no one was transformed, and openness meant simply accepting the established roles for the various members of the community. Parts of chapter 12 can be read to reinforce such a static reading of what it is to be sensitive. But no—this vision is itself a profound vision of transformation. It is realized in struggle, struggle with oneself and also struggle to affirm what we are so that the other may perceive and respect us. Vital ferment is often uncomfortable. Paul was far more open to such ferment than he is often credited with being, and he no doubt brought a great deal of ferment to the church with his message. Our task as interpreters of the caring for one another that is central to this chapter is to be both open to the vision of common life, so important in our time of unreflective individualism, and also to be ready to accept the struggle, and the patience with struggle, that are required if we are to move toward actualizing the vision.

12:31b—13:13 Love as the Highest Gift

The Wisdom Language of Chapter 13

The text shifts rather abruptly from the call to "strive for the greater gifts" to the vision of a "still more excellent way" (12:31). This way or path, of course, is *agape* or love. The chapter is an astonishing poem about *agape*, from the point of view of those who stress that *agape* is God's love. For in this chapter, there is no mention of Christ, nor, in so many words, of God. It is a poem about human love.

The fact that chapter 13 does not speak of Christ arises from its literary form. By choosing a particular traditional way of speaking, Paul was drawn to stay within the limits of what could be said in that kind of language. Though the forms of speech always set limits to what is said, this fact of restriction by the forms of language is all the more striking when language is pushed to its limit, when it is at the margin of what cannot be said, and chapter 13 is an example of language pushed to its limits.

The style and form that Paul adopted in chapter 13 is that of Hellenistic Jewish Wisdom teaching. This was a tradition that tried to focus on the generally human features of behavior, rather than emphasizing the concrete historical circumstances, for instance, of Jewish life. To a considerable degree, this type of Jewish religious speech had absorbed Hellenistic ideas and ways of speaking; in fact, its more speculative forms seem to have been one of the sources of the language of Paul's dialogue partners in Corinth. That Paul chose a style that could so easily have been used by those with whom he was in debate is a sign of the largeness and flexibility of his vision. It is too much to say that he wrote this way in order to meet them on their own ground. But the choice of a wisdom form does show Paul's effort to use a variety of ways of speaking of his deepest concerns. He could not say it all by speaking explicitly of Christ.

The particular literary form of Hellenistic Jewish Wisdom that Paul adopted and used for his praise of love was the form of "praise of a virtue." An example is the praise of truth in 1 Esdras 4:34–40; for instance, "But truth endures and is strong forever, and lives and prevails forever and ever" (verse 38; compare 1 Corinthians 13:8, "love never ends"). Like Paul's "poem," this one (in a much more pedestrian way than 1 Corinthians 13) praises its subject mainly by setting it off against what it is not. (For further examples, see Conzelmann, *First Corinthians*, 219–220.)

Thus though the chapter has great literary power, it is not a hymn and does not connect with the language of worship. (Most early Christian hymns that we know were, in contrast, strongly and explicitly about Christ.) In chapter 13 we are hearing the language of teaching rather than that of worship. The rhythmic power and simplicity of the sentences are directed immediately toward encouraging a form of behavior. The vitality of the appeal, as in the Hellenistic Jewish models, depends in part on presenting the virtue as an acting power in the human situation, almost as personified.

At the same time, Paul adapted this Wisdom style to the purposes of his letter. What could be only a convention of speaking of a virtue in personified terms became in his hands a way of presenting love as an active power, greater than the person who expresses love and yet essentially a part of that person. What was often a formal convention comes alive in a marvelous way.

The interplay of a literary form that usually presented virtues as static qualities to be practiced by those who heard the teaching, with a vision of love as an active power that transcends the power of action of the individual and even transcends the special gifts of the Spirit to the Christian community, is an interplay that is close to the center of Paul's teaching about love. We may say that although elsewhere he speaks of love typically in terms of God and Christ, here he retains the Wisdom form, which speaks of the human situation only, because he believed that love was the deepest intention for humanity.

Concretely, Paul transformed the Wisdom-teaching pattern by bringing it into interaction with the problems at Corinth that 1 Corinthians addressed. Chapter 13 comes rather surprisingly between chapters 12 and 14, which deal with the gifts of the Spirit and largely focus on the community at worship. Some readers believe that the poetic statement about love does not belong here; chapter 14 could follow very naturally directly after chapter 12 without it. Chapter 13 certainly stands by itself and may well have been composed independently, but it also casts a profound light on the issues of chapters 12 and 14. In any case, the passage is a commentary on love specifically in relation to the tensions at Corinth: speaking with tongues, prophesying, giving to the poor, gaining knowledge, and being "puffed up" or arrogant are all themes that connect this section with the letter as a whole. The challenge to a different vision, in which special ecstatic inspiration and special spiritual gifts brought one closest to God, provoked Paul to set forth another way—the way of love, which is not a gift for the privileged few, but a possibility for all—as the orienting center of the Christian vision.

1 CORINTHIANS

The chapter falls into three parts: (1) verses 1–3; (2) verses 4–7; (3) verses 8–13. The first and third parts engage the Corinthian church most concretely. The middle section is the purest example of the Wisdom-teaching form. It is worth noting that in parts one and three the first-person language of "I" appears, but not because Paul was basing his message on his own autobiographical experience (which he did explicitly only when he was pressed into a corner, as in 2 Corinthians 11:16—12:13 and in Galatians 1:11—2:21). Rather, the "I" is a "typical I," an "anyone." Paul did not make direct claims about himself in these sections of 1 Corinthians 13, though we know from other places that he did believe that his behavior expressed the love that he praised here (e.g., 1 Corinthians 16:24, "My love be with all of you in Christ Jesus").

12:31b—13:3 The More Excellent Way

The chapter is introduced by 12:31b: "And I will show you a still more excellent way." "Way" did not mean "manner," but "path," and was a common metaphor for an ethical pattern, of course suggesting the need for choice between paths on which to go; what follows is *the* way or path. The spiritual gifts with which love is contrasted are sometimes spoken of as if they could be chosen, and sometimes as if they were simply given by the Spirit.

The first part (verses 1–3) consists of three "if's"; each one supposes the full possession of one of the great spiritual gifts of chapter 12. "The tongues of mortals and of angels" is not to be pushed for a distinction between two kinds of ecstatic speech (of human beings and angels), but means something like "total possession of ecstatic speech." Without love, this gift, the one most highly prized by some of the Corinthians, is completely without significance. The image of verse 1, the inarticulate gong or cymbal in contrast to articulate speech, shows a contrast to 14:7–9, where the subhuman, inarticulate sound is compared to *uninterpreted* ecstatic speech; here Paul was not concerned with the contrast between interpreted and uninterpreted "tongues," but with the contrast between special gifts and the more fundamental love. This contrast runs throughout the arguments of chapters 13 and 14.

The second "if" combines "prophecy" (inspired preaching), knowledge of "mysteries" (Paul was probably thinking of the mystery, the disclosed secret, of the coming of the end; cf. 15:51), and "knowledge" that was so highly prized by the Corinthians. Again, it is wrong to emphasize distinctions among these terms; they all together signify the special knowledge of God's ways that may come to the believer. To these terms for knowledge is added "faith," in a meaning not usual for Paul (and different from 13:13): faith to move mountains, a capacity of the believer to do unusually powerful things. This was a meaning of faith that had little interest for Paul himself, though he recognized it as an aspect of the life of faith (cf. 12:9). He included this sort of faith to round out the picture of the *unusual* aspects of the special gifts to the believer. Again, without love these most unusual gifts do not make a person "anything."

The third "if" turns to acts of Christian self-giving. It may be that the order of these three types of special gifts represents two reverse orders of valuation, the Corinthians valuing "tongues" the most, and Paul the acts of self-giving. But the main point is that in each case Paul chooses the most extreme examples of the type of gift. They are indeed presented in the order of decreasing value to the audience that Paul has in mind. The acts of self-giving are presented in exaggerated form; in contrast to the giving of 12:28 (continuous attention to the needs of the poor), Paul here speaks about a once-and-for-all giving away, for the poor, of "all my possessions." The meaning of the second illustration, giving away one's body, in the sense of one's very self, is clouded by a puzzling difficulty in the text. The NRSV reads, "so that I may boast" (verse 3). Many older translations, including the RSV, read "to be burned," and the reference is to death by burning. This may refer to martyrdom, when one is compelled by loyalty to faith to give up one's life, but most such challenges came from a later time in the life of the church. It may refer to a dramatic voluntary self-sacrifice, an act somewhat familiar at the time in the stories of Indian wise men who had come to the West and done just this. Such self-immolation is still familiar today in some, particularly Eastern, cultures. But the reading, "that I may boast" or "glory," puts the act of self-giving into a more self-conscious category, and leaves open the question of what happens to "my body." In favor of this reading is the fact that violent death was much more a preoccupation of the church at a later date. The familiar "to be burned" may have been introduced at that time. Against the reading "that I may boast" it can be said that this way of putting it makes unnecessarily explicit what the point is of the whole series, and that the original reading was more likely the bizarre example, "to be burned."

The choice between these two readings does not greatly affect the overall meaning of the section. Gifts and acts that were taken by some in Corinth to be signs of the special presence of the Spirit—ecstatic speaking, inspired knowledge and speaking, and radical self-giving—are nothing without love. The difficult language about "not having love" sounds at first reading as if love were something one could possess, but this implication is not to be pressed. This way of putting it comes from the Wisdom tradition of speaking of ethical acts as if they were existing entities. The sense is the same as saying, "if love is not present."

All three concluding clauses, "I am a noisy gong or a clanging cymbal," "I am nothing," and "I gain nothing," contain the paradox that all these exalted spiritual acts get me nothing if I do them in order to get myself something, yet the very language itself presupposes that it is natural to want to be someone and to get that which makes life meaningful. That is again a Wisdom way of speaking.

13:4–7 Love and Self-Assertion

The second part of the chapter (verses 4–7) characterizes love by setting it over against a whole series of self-assertive acts. In a typical Pauline pattern (A, B, A'), which returns to the beginning after going a separate way in the middle portion, the passage begins with two positive statements ("love is patient; love is kind"), then lists a group of negatives, then returns to the positive in conclusion. Verse 6 with its combination of negative and positive skillfully makes the transition.

Being "patient and kind" is frequently said to be characteristic of both God and of believers, elsewhere in the Bible. Then follow the negatives. These, though they come from a very different tradition from that of the lists of "vices" he gives elsewhere, are shaped by Paul, like those lists, to put special emphasis on acts of aggression and quarreling that set one person over against another (cf. the lists in Romans 1:29–31; Galatians 5:19–21). The final statement, "It bears all things, believes all things, hopes all things, endures all things" (verse 7), is a little obscure, since the first term, "bears," is an unusual one, and its exact force is not certain. It is possible that the series is intended to move in the direction of less and less possible mutual interchange, down to the point where there is nothing left that one can do but endure. Some interpreters (especially Karl Barth) have made the point that this section sets love, in which God is in action, over against the human; the human is represented by the anger, boasting, reckoning up of grievances, etc., that are expressed in the negatives. This interpretation fits well with what Paul says about human behavior elsewhere, for instance in Romans 1 and 2. But here Paul does not make the distinction between the human way and God's way. He remains within the Wisdom language that speaks of human ways of acting, good and bad. We shall have to return later to this question of how God is related to love in view of the chapter as a whole.

13:8–13 Love and the Other Gifts

The third section (verses 8–13) returns to comparison of love with the gifts so highly prized by many of the Corinthians, again in the pattern of A, B, A'. Interestingly, the "I" of the speaker also reappears, though in a different connection from that which was found in the first section. Parts A and A' are also connected by the "quest for something," the quest to be something lasting in the flux of life in the first section, and the quest for a way in which the "I" may endure in the third section. The second section, which on the surface deals with something else, is also strongly connected to this theme by the fact that those types of human behavior that are set over against love are attractive because they seem to offer something lasting to the self.

The language of the third section is in part chosen to fit the Corinthian audience. The "complete" (NRSV; RSV "perfect," verse 10) was one of their favorite terms, and it is likely that "faith, hope, and love" were already familiar to them in this threefold form. However, this section uses the generalized human language of Wisdom throughout to speak of the final end. The hopes of which Paul will speak in the vivid and pictorial language of eschatology a little later on are here presented in more general terms. There is thus a strong correlation between chapters 13 and 15.

The bold thesis of the third section is that what seems to be most ephemeral and transient—the momentary act of self-forgetting love—is an expression of a power that will never give out, and is enduring and eternal in contrast to the great spiritual gifts, which are limited to their temporary function in this age. All the commentators notice this claim, but, astonishingly, few of them speak of how surprising a claim it is. The commentators all suppose that since God is love, love is, of course, eternal. Obvious on one level, this perspective causes the reader to lose sight of the powerful and surprising claim for lastingness of what seems far more elusive and temporary than the great spiritual gifts. What seems the most momentary is truly the lasting reality!

Thus the concluding section is eschatological, dealing with how things will come out in the final end, but Paul casts the eschatological vision in terms of love rather than in terms of Christ. The section begins and ends with the theme of the endurance of love. Verse 8 links this section to the preceding one, which closed with love's power of continual presence. Then prophecy and the gifts of tongues and knowledge, the preeminent signs of divine presence to many Corinthians, are contrasted to love, since they will "come to an end," or "cease," and are "in part," in contrast to the wholeness that will come and is already anticipated by love. The point is made with the illustration of the child who leaves childhood behind, and with the image of the mirror with its indirect, and hence puzzling, vision in contrast to seeing reality directly. Though God is not mentioned expressly anywhere in the chapter, the final contrast, "Now I know only in part; then I will know fully, even as I have been fully known," expresses the prior initiative of God by the use of the passive voice (I have been known by God).

In the final verse, if Paul was using a combination of faith, hope, and love already known to his audience, we should not struggle too much with the question of just how he thought that faith and hope would continue in the perfect coming existence. It is true that elsewhere he speaks of their being temporary (of faith, 2 Corinthians 5:7; of hope, Romans 8:24–25). After all, "faith" itself is used in two different senses in this very chapter (verses 2 and 13), and here Paul distinguished love from the gifts of the Spirit, while in Galatians 5:22 love is one of the fruits of the Spirit. All this shows that we are not dealing with a carefully thought-out theological vocabulary and system, but with a much more direct and metaphorical way of speaking of these matters.

Preaching and Teaching on 1 Corinthians 13

What is the relation of chapter 13 to Paul's usual way of speaking of love as God's love in Christ (as in Romans 5)? The pattern of love is exactly the same in both cases. It is not too much to say that for Paul, it is only through Christ's love that we are set free from ourselves and come to be able to love. It is in passages that speak of God's love in Christ that Paul made his clearest statements about the way in which love disregards the value of the person who is loved—"while we still were sinners Christ died for us" (Romans 5:8b). Love is a gift that comes from beyond ourselves. Human love is freed and enabled by God's love in Christ, and is a derivative love.

How does it happen, then, that Paul says nothing of this in 1 Corinthians 13? The clue is that he was speaking to a Christian community. The community itself had its standing, its very existence, only from the powers that derived from Christ. All this was simply presupposed in chapter 13, though it is very explicit in the letter as a whole. Chapter 13 starts from the question, "What are these powers on which the community is founded, and how are they to be ranked?" To answer such questions, Paul wrote of the centrality of love, indeed of love as that which confers the eternal life that Christ confers.

For the modern interpreter, the question to be faced is how to relate Paul's presupposition, that the words about love are addressed to a definite community that derived its powers from Christ, to the present situation where the boundaries of the Christian community are diffuse, and where we recognize the diversity of the sources of the powers that enable us to live. The Wisdom language Paul used assumed that there can and will be a spontaneous human response to the qualities—in this case, love—of which it spoke. Paul assumed the same, in the context of the Christian community. How to bring Paul's sharply focused vision of love into connection with our time, when most of us recognize authentic love that does not think of itself as explicitly connected with Christ, is one of the great challenges that the chapter leaves with the modern reader. If one thinks of Christ as a power pervasively at work in human existence, not only where Christ is explicitly named, the way is open to connect Paul's way of presenting love with an honest recognition of the pervasive traces of love in our own time.

129

If we turn to the question, "What is the relation between chapter 13 and chapter 15?" which deals with the future in terms of the resurrection, each chapter in its own way provides a foundation for the specific patterns of behavior dealt with in the bulk of the letter. Though Christ is only implicitly present in chapter 13, it would be correct to say that for Paul, both chapters were ways of showing how Christ is the foundation for concrete patterns of living—the one speaking of renewed patterns of life, the other of the outcome of life.

Chapter 15 works out, in apocalyptic language, a full vision of how our transient, momentary acts of faith and love may be taken up into an order of lasting significance. If this is not an important question—if love can be adequately spoken of as a momentary encounter—then we will choose chapter 13 as the true foundation of what Paul says about Christian behavior. But if we find that continuity in time is an inescapable aspect of Christian behavior and of love, then we will have to say that chapters 13 and 15 complement each other to give a foundational vision on which to base Christian behavior. To me it is important that, even though no specific outcome can be guaranteed, the "outcome" is important for love, so that chapter 15 has to work with chapter 13 in the overall vision. The reason is found in the nature of love itself: even though it is actual only in the moment, and cannot be absorbed into a merely habitual form of behavior, love does inevitably reach into the future, since the future of the other is a concern of love as well as the other's well-being in this moment in which one acts.

Next, we turn to the question of whether and how love is "my act," a thoroughly human activity. The chapter, especially in its central second part, speaks of love as an acting power. This way of putting it was a convention within the Wisdom tradition that Paul here followed. It expresses the powerful faith that love is a power that somehow transcends the individual person. If this insight is joined to those passages where Paul spoke of love as God's love, toward which the human being can be only receptive (such as Romans 3:21–26; 5:6–11; and all that Paul says about "works"), then it is possible to think that love is not really "my act." "I know that nothing good dwells within me" (Romans 7:18). Love, then, would be only God at work; of this working I am a receptive vehicle. If we have to contrast human activity as the effort to control the environment and other people, with human receptivity that allows us to be open to the divine presence, then the life of faith will be pure receptivity, and there will be no element of active human creativity in it.

But this way of thinking simply does not fit the text. Here the human person is not receptive, but active in a transformed way. Love is contrasted with ordinary human ways, and linked to God by its connection with what endures; but it is also fully "my act," the act of the person who responds in this way. That Paul chose this Wisdom language to speak of love is a sign that he could not say everything about Christian faith in the language of being receptive.

Paul so drastically transformed the language of the description of a virtue that he spoke of the "beyond in the midst," to use a phrase of Dietrich Bonhoeffer's. Numerous modern readers and theologians who have been alienated from the traditional language about God have found in the presentation of love in this chapter (and elsewhere in the New Testament) a new entry into the question of God and the transcendent, now a transcendent that is both fully my act and a power given from beyond myself. One could well speak of this chapter as a qualitative way of speaking of the transcendent. But it would have to be said at the same time that for Paul and for 1 Corinthians the chapter was not isolated, but found its strength in its relation to other ways of speaking of the transcendent or God.

If these ways are difficult for some modern readers, we may rejoice that they find entry into the question of God in chapter 13. However, from the point of view of the letter as a whole, the vision of this chapter is by no means a new one, but has deep roots in the Hebrew Scriptures, as well as in the proclamation about Christ. The task of integrating the vision of self-forgetful love as an immanent transforming power into a larger framework in which God can be spoken of in other ways is never easy, and it is particularly difficult in our time. First Corinthians offers a model of such integration, an integration centered on the figure of Christ, even though Christ is not mentioned in this chapter.

In this text Paul did not grapple with the question of how generous love, which asks nothing for itself (*agape*), and the love of longing or desire, which is a movement toward what does have value (*eros*), are related to each other. Many classic treatments of this contrast have made the two loves as different as possible. They are different. The contrast is a fruitful one for our thinking and our imagination.

But ask yourself the question: does Paul's great chapter on love have nothing to do with how friends or people who love each other or married couples get along with each other? Of course it does! It cannot be the whole story, because all these relationships fulfill *needs* that are not in view in the chapter on love.

What Paul does is to bring *agape* so thoroughly into the human world that it can be, so to speak, a conversation partner with the other kinds of love. He pictures our own engagement in love, and sets it in relation to the concrete problems that we— or to be exact, the Corinthians—live through, in such a way that we cannot escape its being a real possibility, something that can really come to pass in our lives. The deep engagement and interaction of love with all the energies of life means, as Christians have often been reluctant to admit, that there is no wholly unambiguous love. Love is always interwoven with claims for power, for instance, in ways of which the lover is often unconscious. Nevertheless, generous love is possible and real.

This is why chapter 13 plays so central a role in bringing the vision of 1 Corinthians into dialogue with the present time. What Paul says elsewhere about *agape* is foundational—that it comes from God, that it is God's love, that the cross of Christ has actualized it in our Christian history in a decisive way. We need that foundation that comes to expression, for instance, in chapter 1 of this letter.

But chapter 13 gives us the other side, the picture of how love enters into the common life, how though it is God's love it is also our love, which can enter into conversation with and give direction to the energies of our lives, including our erotic or romantic love.

These other energies do come from God and are good, although they are so powerful that we may find it hard to hold them in a harmonious whole. We cannot simply impose *agape* upon them. They have their own importance and their own integrity. But in Christian faith we discover that the truest clue to how we belong together and give to each other is the love that Paul so powerfully describes in the chapter. There is, as Paul says, a diversity of gifts, but this one is open to all of us—its often inconspicuous, humble, and yet spontaneous acts can give meaning and depth to the whole of life, and give direction to the very necessary self-expression and assertion of our needs that the other kinds of love, by their nature, express.

14:1–40 Being Carried Beyond Oneself *versus* Understanding and Sharing

The central thrust of chapter 14 is very clear: in worship it is good for a person to pour out a deeply felt faith by "speaking in tongues," that is, by the outpouring of unintelligible speech. But it is better to speak intelligibly in worship, so that those who hear may be challenged to expand their understanding and commitment—and thus the church as a whole will be "built up," will be woven together and strengthened in mutual sharing of life and faith.

Earlier, Paul had urged the group to be thankful for the particular gift or gifts each one had been given by the Spirit. The emphasis was on growing in mutual acceptance of varied people and gifts, and recognizing the value of each (chapter 12). Then chapter 13 struck a different note, offering a vision of a "still more excellent way" (12:31) toward which anyone could aim, no matter what particular gifts one was able to exercise. The note of choosing and striving, not simply accepting what has already been experienced as given, carries forward throughout chapter 14. Thus the whole discussion of spiritual gifts opens the way to reflection about the interaction between receiving, simply accepting life as a gift, and choosing, making an effort to reach toward a fuller experience.

The chapter moves through a series of exhortations and illustrations, reiterating the same point from different perspectives. As is often the case, the thought of the thematic sentence at the beginning is repeated in a different form at the end (14:1, 39–40).

The unifying thread that links the various comments is the theme of "building up" the church, of recognizing one's relatedness to the whole and putting one's gifts to work not just for one's own growth or benefit, but for the strengthening and deepening of the interrelatedness of the whole. Paul expected this result from "prophecy," which did not mean foretelling the future, but is much closer to what we mean by "preaching"— although the note of direct inspiration by the Spirit was much stronger as both Paul and the Corinthians thought about "prophecy" than is the case with our view of preaching.

1 CORINTHIANS

14:1–5 Ecstatic Speaking and Benefiting the Church

The chapter opens a bit awkwardly because it has to relate back both to chapter 13 on love and to chapter 12 on the gifts of the Spirit. As already noted, the theme of *acting* in relation to what God does, not just receiving it, carries forward from chapter 13 and contrasts this presentation of the gifts of the Spirit with the first discussion of them in chapter 12. (Note 14:1, "pursue," "strive.")

Then the main point of the whole chapter is briefly stated: speaking in tongues helps the one who speaks; prophecy helps the whole church. We shall have to reflect in our concluding section on whether this distinction, so clear to Paul, is wholly adequate. In any case, both functions are recognized as genuinely inspired.

"Speaking in tongues" was and is the outpouring of unintelligible speech, which is felt by the speaker and the congregation as an inspired gift, a sign of the presence—we may say, the direct presence—of God's Spirit. This particular form of ecstatic experience, of being carried beyond oneself, was shaped in the Corinthian church by similar experiences in other religions of the time, as religious experience is always shaped by the possibilities available in the stream of culture in which it occurs. Typically, in the culture of the time, being carried away ecstatically was taken to mean that one's self was temporarily set aside by the incoming presence of a divine spirit. The language poured out was unintelligible because the Spirit opened the way to things beyond ordinary understanding. In such ecstatic experience, it was thought that the person receiving the presence of a spirit or the Spirit was not in control; the genuineness of the inspiration was believed to be verified by the way in which the receiver felt powerless to shape what was said. As the chapter develops, we shall see that Paul modified this way of thinking.

Since ecstatic speech was not intelligible, someone often interpreted what was spoken. Paul insisted that for ecstatic speech to be fruitful for the assembly, there *must be* an interpretation of it. Sometimes the text speaks as if a second person might do this (14:5, "unless some one interprets"; 14:28), but when Paul speaks directly to a person inspired to speak in tongues, the assumption is that this same person should also interpret (14:13, "one who speaks in a tongue should pray for the power to interpret"). Some of those who spoke in tongues very likely resisted this advice; they may have felt that the depth of what they experienced could not be carried over into ordinary speech.

14:6–12 Examples of No Communication

Music that has no form cannot communicate, says Paul. Perhaps we could say that musical sounds that do not fit into any recognized genre or musical type are unable to evoke our response. More specifically, a trumpet call to battle must be given in a form already known.

Similarly, it is futile to try to communicate if we do not share a language. These homely illustrations reinforce the point that communication, interchange, is the heart of worship. Paul holds that the ecstatic does not contribute to this.

14:13–19 The Importance of Interpreting

The logical conclusion of what has been said so far is that if a person is to let the Spirit's inspiration break forth in ecstatic speech, it is important also to be given the power to interpret what one says ecstatically. The point is made by separating the "mind," which understands a prayer or a song, from the "spirit," which produces sounds that cannot be understood by others. We should not press the dualistic separation of mind and spirit too far. By "mind" Paul points to those faculties that enable us to communicate, so that the "outsider" will be able to say "Amen" to what one has said (verse 16; on the "outsider" see 14:20–25).

The "I" of this paragraph is at first a general one, an "anyone": "I will sing praise with the spirit, but I will sing praise with the mind also" (verse 15b). Toward the end the text shifts to a very personal "I": "I thank God that I speak in tongues more than all of you" (verse 18). Paul commits himself to this form of worship thoroughly, but goes on at once to say that he would far rather speak a few words "with my mind," to "instruct others" than to speak endless words in "a tongue." He does not mention interpreting his own ecstatic speech, but rather of shifting to a different mode of taking part in worship.

14:20–25 How the Outsider Responds

The next illustration of the two forms of speaking reveals to us that "unbelievers" were frequent participants in the worship of the community. What Paul says is at first sight puzzling, for he says that "tongues...are a sign not for believers but for unbelievers" (verse 22), but goes on to say that an unbeliever will be thrown off by speaking in tongues, and will not come to believe, while if the members of the congregation "prophesy," an unbeliever or outsider will "bow down before God and worship" (verses 24–25). Here Paul draws on a rich prophetic tradition about signs that are negative and prevent the hearer from understanding (as in his reading of the text he quotes, Isaiah 28:11–12; for negative signs see especially Isaiah 6:9–13). Rather than expose the outsiders who visit the church to such a destructive result, he would limit ecstatic speech, and encourage the intelligible speaking to which one may hope that the newcomers will respond. The "unbelievers" are inquirers who have not yet accepted faith in Christ. The "outsiders" may be similar, or may simply be people who do not share the ecstatic experience of the Spirit.

14:26–33a A Picture of the Church at Worship

The preceding two paragraphs have already given important clues to the way in which Paul thought worship should take place. We hear of the "outsider" who is expected to respond with an "Amen" in verse 16, and of unbelievers who may come to believe, if they are not disconcerted by ecstatic speech, in verses 20–25. Now Paul sketches a picture of worship, a very flexible procedure where anyone may offer "a hymn, a lesson, a revelation, a tongue, or an interpretation" (verse 26). Speaking in worship is to be open to anyone, but each is to be attentive to the good of all, to "building up." If any speak in tongues, it is to be only a few, and only if someone can interpret. A speaker is to give place to another who has something given to him or her to say (on women speaking, see on 14:33b–36). Most revealing is the final statement, that "the spirits of prophets are subject to the prophets, for God is a God not of disorder but of peace" (verses 32–33). In contrast to some views of inspiration, Paul asserts that the "spirit" does not take total control. The message comes from the Spirit, but the one receiving it is able to decide about how to present it.

The language here ("the spirits of prophets," verse 32) is drawn from a tradition in which each prophetic voice was given by a particular spirit. This language should not be pressed to contrast with Paul's fundamental conviction that all inspiration came from the one Spirit of God. The whole chapter holds together two convictions: first, that a single source, the Spirit,

136

or, ultimately, God, is responsible for all true inspiration, and second, that the concrete expressions of inspired speech will be quite varied, depending on the particular person and that person's gifts or capacities.

What a revealing glimpse of a vital community, whose worship was in good measure unstructured, open to participation by all, and guided not by a pre-set program, but by the Spirit! No wonder that the meetings were often boisterous and no wonder that several voices were often heard at once. Apparently there was no one who regularly presided, in contrast to the almost universal practice of the later church. Paul's plan for a more sober worship is not an administrative reform, but a plea for mutual consideration, so that the whole group may be "built up."

Though the following statement confronts a difficulty in the very next section (see below), it is probable that many of the prophets and ecstatic speakers were women. To be able to speak in public, to be leaders in a group, to experience the direct inspiration of the Spirit—all were new and liberating experiences for most of them, experiences that gave women a new status and dignity that was sadly lacking for them in the patriarchal society of the time. We may be confident that at times they were impatient with Paul for his insistence on proper order, for they prized the spontaneity they were discovering. At the same time, we believe that Paul was much more on their side, more deeply committed to the church as a nonhierarchical society, than some recent scholars understand him to have been. (See the study of Antoinette Wire, *The Corinthian Women Prophets*.)

14:33b–36 Women Are Not to Speak

Though the immediately preceding verses placed no restriction on any class of speaker by virtue of class, this short statement completely denies to "women" the right to speak in the assembly. "Women" is placed in quotation marks to remind the reader that in Greek the same word means both "woman" and "wife." The text goes on to say that women may ask their husbands at home, if there is anything that they want to know. Thus if the statement is to be taken narrowly, it is addressed to married women.

Often in Greek literature we hear how excellent it is for women to be quiet and listen. The advice of this section would have been recognized as the usual middle-class custom by many men in the world of Paul. Evidently many women in the Corinthian church did not accept any such restriction. Earlier in 1 Corinthians, in 11:2–16, Paul had fully recognized the right and the propriety of women speaking in Christian worship—although he had tried to lay down some very firm rules about how they should appear when they did so. Here the letter takes a position which directly conflicts with 11:2–16. How are we to understand the conflict?

Various theories have been suggested. Some recent interpreters hold that Paul here denied married women the right to speak in public, for that would have been too much of a disturbance of the patriarchal marriage patterns of the day, while in chapter 11 he had been speaking of unmarried women, who were at least to some degree free from the social restrictions placed upon wives. Paul recognized their greater freedom by agreeing with their claim to speak. This way of harmonizing the two statements has the great merit of bringing to the reader's attention the freedom that women could attain by staying out of marriage—a point that had escaped most male interpreters. (For this view, see Elisabeth Schüssler Fiorenza, *In Memory of Her*, 230–233). The problem with this interpretation is that there is no indication in 11:2–16 that the text is dealing only with unmarried women; the assumption that a woman could ask her husband may represent simply a thoughtless male presupposition that adult women were married. Certainly this section does not suggest that unmarried women could speak. Paul's own situation is better reflected in the way in which married couples, working together, appear not infrequently in Paul's letters in the building up of the church (for instance, Aquila and Prisca in 16:19; granted, there is nothing said about women speaking).

Another way of reading the contradiction is to say that in chapter 11 Paul was leading up to this passage, restricting women, so to speak, by degrees, but saying here what he really thought. But it is not really possible to think of Paul as speaking in such a deceptive manner in 11:2–16, if he planned to go on and write 14:33b–36. The only possibility of reading the two passages this way is to say that they were written at two different times, and that Paul had changed his mind (in which direction?). Many writers think that 1 Corinthians is made up from pieces that Paul wrote at different times, but we have noted above that it makes better sense to take the present letter as a whole.

A third possibility has recently come to receive attention: verses 33b–35, which forbid women to speak, are a quotation from certain Corinthians who patriarchally believe that women should not be heard; verse 36 is Paul's sharp rejection of this position (rather than his rejection of the claim of women to speak, as it has usually been taken). This is a very appealing suggestion. But it presupposes that Paul's letter is even more of a patchwork of statements than we have taken it to be. Even more important, the language, especially with the reference to "all the churches" (verse 33b) and to what the law says (verse 34), sounds more like a church rule set by tradition than a recently formulated Corinthian opinion.

Thus here we follow a fourth possibility, advocated by many scholars for many years. These verses were not originally part of 1 Corinthians. The movement is very easy from 14:33a to 14:37, both of which speak of "prophecy." There is no clear-cut evidence in the history of the copying of 1 Corinthians that this passage is a later addition. (Some copies do place verses 34–35 after verse 40, and it is barely possible that this shift reflects a version of the letter which did not contain this passage; the displacement would be a result of adding these verses at the end, in making a new copy of the letter, by copying them from the margin of the manuscript from which the scribe was working, in which they had been noted down from another version of the letter in which they had already been added. But it is much more likely that the shift in position was the result of some copyist's feeling that these verses broke the line of thought rather abruptly.)

The reasons for taking these verses as an addition to the letter are strong. Unless one distinguishes two classes of women (a distinction not made clear by the text), this passage contradicts what is said earlier, in chapter 11. Further, the style and language are similar to what we read in writing from a slightly later time in the church, when fixed rules had come to replace the flexibility of the early days. There is a fairly close parallel to 14:33b–36 in 1 Timothy 2:11–12, which comes from a later time in spite of being attributed to Paul, and which may indeed have provided the model for these words. The passive voice, "they are not permitted to speak" (14:34; literally, "it is not permitted [to] them to speak" [KJV]) is more suitable in a church rule than in a direct statement by Paul. It is untypical for Paul to appeal to "the law."

139

Thus we take the position that the passage that forbids women to speak was not written by Paul, but was added later when a more authoritarian church compelled women to conform to the middle-class propriety of the day.

14:37–40 A Final Admonition to Follow Paul

The closing admonition, like the one in chapter 11 that closes the discussion of how women are to speak, is formed to emphasize Paul's authority. Here the preceding discussion of prophecy leads to the thought that what Paul has been urging, which is itself a prophetic utterance, will be recognized by other prophets as valid.

Preaching and Teaching on
1 Corinthians 14

Charismatic churches are probably the fastest growing part of the Christian church, while the churches for which this book is written are seeking a better vision of their purpose. Thus we will do well to take seriously the style of worship upon which Paul here reflects. Speaking in tongues brings emotional intensity, indeed the outpouring of unconscious levels of experience, into the worship of the community in ways not typical either of traditional liturgies or of services focused on the word. That God speaks to us through these levels is something we need to rediscover. Charismatic churches give dignity and depth to the lives of many who would not find themselves at home in the more staid worship that is familiar to most of those who will read this book. If it is true that such experience brings with it both the danger of thinking oneself on a higher level than those who do not have it, and the danger of excluding social responsibility from the scope of one's faith, then the cautions of Paul can serve to correct and broaden the life of the charismatic communities.

American Christianity is struggling to move beyond an individualistic piety that has not helped to build community, either in the church or in the wider society. The whole point of chapter 14 is that we do belong together far more deeply than we often realize. We do not simply contribute to one another's lives from the outside, but we are mutually formed as we grow together—a point already made especially in chapters 8—10. The specific illustration that carries the point here is not a current issue in most churches, but the basic point is one to which every thoughtful reader will come back again and again. We can really receive and use the gifts we have been given only as we let them flow into the interchange, the give-and-take, by which the network of life and community is enlarged and strengthened. This chapter is a focal statement of the theme we have highlighted for the whole letter: finding faith in community.

We must not lose sight of this basic point. It is an important one because a focus of consciousness upon an intense spiritual experience in any culture can easily suppress an awareness of mutual belonging. It may also lead to a feeling of superiority over those whose experience is more low-key. We could extract from Paul's whole discussion the motto: No deepening of the spiritual life without engagement in society; no engagement of faith in society without a deepening of the spiritual life.

At the same time, we must ask whether the issue dealt with here is an altogether happy illustration of the point. Paul presents the ecstatic speaker as an individual whose outpouring of faith, guided by the Spirit, will benefit no one else. This was hardly the case, as a visit to a Holiness church in the Appalachian Mountains or to many a church outside the main-line of middle-class Christianity would show. Intense emotion is deeply shared and communicated in such services of worship, and no doubt it was in Corinth as well. That was precisely why several people began to speak at once. Those who respond to God's presence in quieter ways will do well to respect such passionate expressions of the nearness and the "weight" of God's presence, and to recognize the strong element of shared experience in such worship. It is not just individualism, and if Paul interpreted it in that way, he saw only one side of it. Those who spoke in tongues were building up the church in their own way.

It has been suggested that many of those who prophesied and spoke in tongues were women who were celebrating their freedom to take part in worship, and were more relaxed about spontaneous and somewhat disorganized worship than Paul was. This may well be true, and if so, we see another reminder of how hard it is to reach toward a truly open community. To move toward it requires both imagination and patience on the part of all, but also the willingness to speak up and claim one's place on the part of those who are not yet recognized as full participants. The issue between Paul's "all things should be done decently and in order" (verse 40) and the move toward a more spontaneous and expressive worship can thus be seen as part of the long struggle in the church to make a place for all the voices that speak in the community—a struggle in which Paul was truly a leader although he often, as here, only partly heard the voice that was struggling to be heard.

Speaking in tongues was regarded by many in Corinth as the definitive mark of the Spirit. Paul insists that it is only one of many gifts. Though speaking in tongues is still practiced in many churches, and has been recovered as a form of Christian worship in our own time, it is only one form of intensely felt presence of the Spirit. In our world and in our churches, for many people it may well be forms of meditation, largely learned directly or indirectly from Hinduism and Buddhism, that will be rough equivalents to speaking in tongues for Corinth. They are typical ways of concentrating the self and opening it to the power that is beyond it. They often appear to be "the real thing" in a way that "ordinary" worship does not. They are to be recognized and encouraged as authentic forms of spirituality, just as speaking in tongues is to be recognized, even though an adequate understanding of the transformation of consciousness through meditation will require other images besides the presence of the Spirit.

Paul's judgments would be applicable to these newer forms of spirituality as well. Their claims to an element direct awareness of the ultimate mystery can be recognized. Yet there is no unambiguous ecstasy, just as there is no unambiguous love. Not only is each form, immediate as it seems, shaped by the cultural situation in which it is expressed; each form also carries the possibility of being used to evade responsibility and to grasp for power. Paul's whole treatment of the extraordinary and the less striking gifts of the Spirit stands as an enduring vantage point from which to assess the strengths and weaknesses of our modern quests as well as those of the Corinthians.

15:1-58 THIRD MAIN SECTION OF "SPECIFIC ISSUES":

The Resurrection

With chapter 15, the topic shifts somewhat abruptly from the forms of the community's life to the basis that makes that life possible. This basis is the resurrection, which, taken with the already-present gift of Christ, provides a framework in which the lives and acts of believers are given enduring meaning. The repeated not "in vain" or not "futile" (verses 1–2, 10, 14, 17, 58, with related phrases elsewhere) furnishes the fundamental link with what has gone before. The specific topic of the resurrection of the body connects this chapter with 6:12–20, while the "bad company ruins good morals" of 15:33 links back to 10:1–22; but the broader connection lies in the promise that the commitment and style of the life of faith are taken up into an enduring future. Paul writes more as a pastor than as a speculative thinker, as is rightly seen by David W. Kuck, *Judgment and Community Conflict*, 256.

The resurrection is presented in two sections: (1) a traditional creedal statement about the resurrection of Christ, expanded by Paul (15:1–11), and (2) a long essay, poetic in parts, though in a very different way from chapter 13, about the resurrection of all believers, which is still in the future (15:12–58). The two parts are linked by the conviction that Christ's resurrection is the initiating point of the resurrection of believers, and thus if this latter resurrection is brought into question, the foundation of the Christian faith in the resurrection of Christ is also undermined.

We cannot examine all the issues raised in the enormous literature about this wonderful chapter. We shall focus on questions that point forward to how one may understand this visionary chapter in the very different world in which we live.

15:1–11 A Traditional Creed Applied

The resurrection of Christ had been at the heart of the message that Paul had preached, and he begins by quoting an already established formulation of Christian belief to remind his hearers that they had from the beginning heard and accepted this tradition. Of course, the tradition included both the death and the resurrection of Jesus, though here attention is turned to the resurrection, in contrast to earlier settings where Paul had emphasized only the death of Jesus (2:2, etc.). After a sharp reminder that unless they hold fast to the tradition they will have believed for nothing, Paul repeats, expands, and applies the confession of faith that he had received.

Christ died and was raised (verses 3–5); the two phases of Christ's coming are guaranteed both by the fulfillment of scripture ("in accordance with the scriptures," 15:3, 4), and by observation or experience ("he was buried" [15:4]; "he appeared to Cephas [Peter], then to the twelve" [15:5]). It may well be that the particular passages of the Hebrew Scriptures that established the place of Jesus' death and resurrection in God's design had not yet been definitely specified.

Paul received the list of appearances that follows (verses 6–8) from various traditions (except, of course, the appearance to himself), but it is likely that the original statement ended with the appearances to Peter and the twelve. These other appearances, "to more than five hundred brothers and sisters at one time" (some of whom have died, even though they had seen the Lord), to James (the brother of Jesus), and to "all the apostles," were gathered in traditions different from those that are recorded in the Gospels, as is also the case with the first appearances to Peter and the twelve. It is not possible to bring all of these traditions into harmony. The death of Jesus was a great problem to the early Christians, and they paid great attention to it and carefully arranged its story; the resurrection was so clear to their experience that little thought was given to classifying and organizing the traditions about it. We cannot here enter into the fascinating questions that this section raises about these resurrection traditions and about the question of whom Paul considered to be apostles.

We should note that in contrast to the resurrection narratives in the Gospels, Paul's traditions do not include appearances to women, except insofar as the "more than five hundred brothers and sisters" (verse 6, NRSV, literally, "more than five hundred brothers") included women. Paul may have edited his traditions to omit women, but it is more likely that his sources included only appearances to men (except as noted above).

As we have seen earlier, a general statement about the Christian message often leads Paul to inject his own special role into the discourse. Here the appearance to Paul, "last of all" (verse 8), serves the double purpose of making clear that no more such appearances are to be expected, and of reaffirming Paul's own authority, which is the more powerful because it arises from a reversal: he had persecuted the church of God (verse 9). (On what Paul says here in relation to other statements about his apostleship, see the section on "Paul as Apostle," above, pp. 42–45). The section closes with the emphatic statement that he and "they," that is, the other apostles, had proclaimed the same message, the message of Christ's resurrection.

It is in keeping with what Paul says later about the resurrection of believers (verses 35–57) that Christ appeared to Paul as a transformed being, not as a flesh-and-blood appearance. Paul assumed that all the appearances were of this kind.

Though Paul is clear that these decisive appearances have come to an end, we should not lose sight of the way in which the living Christ or the Spirit continued to be a vivid and vital presence in the church.

15:12–28 The Necessity of the Resurrection

The resurrection of Christ was the accepted basis of faith both for Paul and for the Corinthians. No one seems to have questioned it. But from what Paul says in verse 12 it appears that some in Corinth did question the reality of a future resurrection. ("How can some of you say there is no resurrection of the dead?") Paul grapples with this question first by referring back to the tradition he has just cited: if there is no such reality as the resurrection, then Christ has not been raised. The field of force that they believe has transformed their lives is illusory ("you are still in your sins" [verse 17]). Further, the apostles, including Paul, are falsifiers of God's truth, and those believers

145

who have already died have not been transformed to new life. Without the coming transformation of the resurrection, "we are of all people most to be pitied" (verse 19).

Leaving this hypothetical argument, the text turns to a strong positive affirmation: "But in fact Christ has been raised from the dead, the first fruits of those who have died" (verse 20). Thus the resurrection of Christ and the resurrection of believers are inextricably linked; Christ is the "first fruits" or early harvest sacrifice that announces the full harvest that is soon to come. Paul expands this basic conviction by setting it in a narrative about the end, a narrative that draws on tradition although he no doubt gave it his own emphasis. But this tradition is very different from the one with which the chapter opens; it is an explanation of the faith rather than a basic confession.

Two elements of this narrative appear later in the chapter. One is the contrast between Adam and Christ, a contrast between two kinds of human existence (15:21–22, compare 15:45–49; Romans 5:12–21). The life initiated by Adam is broken and transient; that springing from Christ is the fulfillment of all that human life is intended to be. The other item is the turning point of the narrative: death is overcome (15:26; compare 15:54–57). It does not matter that some have already died; they will be renewed to life in the resurrection since death will be eliminated.

Probably here and throughout chapter 15 Paul's thought is more fluid than it has often been taken to be. What is most striking about the story of Christ's victory is that, in contrast to most such visions of the end, Paul pays no attention to the fate of those who do not believe. A prime stimulus to the development of the image of a final end was the longing for justice, a longing that bad people get what they deserve. This motivation, and the image of a last judgment, are lacking here, except as the destruction "every ruler and every authority and power" (verse 24) implies judgment. Paul is concerned with the future as gift. Of course the gift has ethical consequences; that is why it is placed at the climax of the letter.

The language of struggle, which in other writers expresses the hope for punishment of the wicked, here serves to express confidence that those pervasive, destructive forces that hamper and destroy life will at last be eliminated. The profoundest of these forces is death (verse 26).

The narrative of the end closes with the surprising move that ultimately Christ will return to God the authority that makes

Christ's function possible (verses 27–28). God will be "all in all" (NRSV) or "God will rule completely over all" (TEV, verse 28). How Paul envisioned the condition in which there would be no opposition to God is not clear. A modern reader may think of a final dissolution of all reality into the God from which it all arose—a view that would be congenial with the belief that life after death lasts only until the finite possibilities of each limited individual have been fully developed. But it is far more probable that Paul considered the future to be one in which the particular lives of believers would continue indefinitely ("we will be with the Lord forever," 1 Thessalonians 4:17). At this point, however, his attention is turned not to such questions, but to the vision of an existence in which all will be in harmony with God's purpose.

15:29–34 Practical Implications of the Resurrection

The passionate and poetic vision of a final resolution of all conflict is set aside for a moment (it will reappear toward the end of the chapter), so that two short comments can be made about the practical consequences of faith in the resurrection. The first of these is a puzzle. Paul speaks of "those…who receive baptism on behalf of the dead" (verse 29). Such persons would be deceiving themselves if the dead are not raised. Attempts have been made to explain "baptism on behalf of the dead" as really something else, for instance, the baptism of one's own mortal body. But the language is clear, and means baptism for someone else, who has died. That some at Corinth could do this shows that they did not deny all forms of survival after death, but to Paul, meaningful survival with Christ could be possible only through the resurrection of the body.

If this practice seems strange to the modern reader, that is because we do not have the strong sense of the interconnectedness of life that enabled Paul to accept it even though he did not encourage it. A similar, though nonsacramental, practice that has also been the focus of much controversy is prayer on behalf of the dead. No matter what theologians may say, this kind of prayer seems right and inevitable to many if not most Christians, whether or not they are clear about just what kind of difference it can make. The powerful inclination toward it can cast light on what seems and is a very strange Corinthian practice.

More important is the next illustration, which draws together Paul's own single-hearted commitment and willingness to take risks with a wider picture of the grounding of right action in the confidence that what we do is not forgotten. Here again, the pastoral consequences of faith in the resurrection are in the focus. Paul and all the rest can know that their commitment and action have results. Otherwise, Paul claims, there would be no point in moral action. We do not know just what risks of his own Paul was writing about when he spoke of fighting with beasts at Ephesus (verse 32).

"Let us eat and drink, for tomorrow we die" (quoted from Isaiah 22:13), an absurdity to Paul, reflects a wisdom or commonsense tradition that is here set in a framework of apocalyptic expectation. This quotation leads to an even more general ethical warning that wrong actions have inevitable consequences, in which Paul quotes the Greek poet Menander, "Bad company ruins good morals" (verse 33). The section ends with a very general appeal to do what is right.

15:35–49 Resurrection as Transformation

The main point of this dense and complex section is very clear. Those who belong to Christ will be given a new form of concrete existence by God's gift in Christ's final victory. To make his point Paul draws both on rather general wisdom thinking— human insight—and on a speculative tradition about Adam, here linked to Christ, the details of which are imperfectly known to us.

The most important thing to observe is that Paul's message about the radical transformation of existence is cast in language that draws on the human ability to understand the world around us. Even this marvelous transformation will be part of a creation that is held together by the wisdom of God, a wisdom that we can recognize as we look back to the world from the point of view of faith. Similarly, in chapter 13 wisdom language is used to speak of the transformation, through agape or love, of life in the present existence.

Paul presupposed that for human beings to exist they have to be in a "body," a concrete form. His argument is shaped to convince those who doubt that a "body" is possible after death. The commentators rightly point out that this section strongly emphasizes the break between "now" and the new life that is to come. This new life is not something that simply unfolds from our present existence. The metaphor of the seed (verses 36–38) could easily mean that to a modern person, but Paul's point is that the new life is simply a gift from God ("But God gives it [the seed] a body as [God] has chosen" [verse 38]).

The Adam/Christ contrast sets the first stage, the "physical" (NRSV, literally, "psychical" or soul-animated) body over against the "spiritual" body or spirit-animated body that is given through Christ. On Adam and Christ, see also 15:21–22. It is clear that the biblical story of Adam has been read from the point of view of a mythical picture of the first human being, for Genesis 2:7, which speaks simply of Adam or man becoming a living being, is here quoted in an expanded form that speaks of a *"first* man, Adam"; so that an added clause can contrast this first man with the "last Adam" (Christ). The original creation, which we know in experience is a terribly broken one, will be replaced by a new existence that can only be described indirectly as it is in this intense paragraph.

Binding the different metaphors together is the underlying conviction that what is renewed is not just a shadowy or ghostly remnant of the person, a soul, as Paul seems to have believed that some of the Corinthians thought. Rather, a real "spirit-controlled" or "spirit-animated" body, a body that embodies the whole person and is still a means of communication, will be given in the new life. All this will be possible because the believer is and will be a part of the new humanity of which Christ is the origin ("we will also bear the image of the man of heaven" [verse 49]).

15:50–58 Thanks Be to God!

The poetic intensity to which the preceding paragraph rises at its close is heightened in the final statement, which sums up the whole narrative of the resurrection as a "mystery" (verse 51), a now-revealed secret about the transformation from this perishable existence to the coming imperishable life. Though no longer "flesh and blood" (verse 50), we shall still be "we" (verse 51). The text here draws on the story of the final events, which has already been sketched in verses 20–28, but while the first version of this story spoke of the overcoming of "every ruler and every authority and power" (verse 24), with death as the "last enemy" (verse 26), here the sole focus is on what really interested Paul the most throughout—the overcoming of death (verses 54–57).

The climactic note of joy, expressed in quotations adapted from Isaiah 25:7 (25:8 in many translations) and Hosea 13:14 (verses 54–55), is followed by a skillful shift to the pastoral concern that lies behind the whole teaching about the resurrection. The overcoming of death implies that sin is also overcome, and this in turn means that the law will no longer be the "power" of sin (verse 56). Some interpreters have regarded the mention of the law as an intrusion here, since it has not been mentioned before in this chapter and is not a large issue in the whole letter. But if we understand the law specifically in its sense of being a temptation to set up an elitist boundary for the community—as recent studies have suggested—then the connection with the rest of the letter is clear, and the culminating point of this great vision of the future is that its gift cannot be limited by any elitist human boundaries. This point leads naturally to the final quiet reminder that "in the Lord your labor is not in vain" (verse 58), the labor being above all the labor of building a nonelitist community, which is so central to the whole letter.

Preaching and Teaching on
1 Corinthians 15

1. The Resurrection of Christ

First Corinthians 15 is a powerful, poetic, and visionary statement. How can we most profoundly and honestly recover and reenact the confidence and joy that animate the whole discussion of the resurrection? We need to see the whole statement as poetic, as stretching language to its limits and quickening our imagination, and also see it as a serious statement about reality. Too often interpreters have believed that they had to choose one or the other of these two paths, since they believed that poetry and reality are at a distance from each other.

Many of the images of this chapter cannot simply be repeated in the world of thought and imagination in which we live today. Few would maintain that the "last trumpet" (verse 52, cf. 1 Thessalonians 4:16) is a part of their world of belief. Nor will it work to insist that there is some bare minimum of "facts" that must be held onto if an interpretation is to be a true application of the message of 1 Corinthians 15 to the world of today. We will do far better to let these powerful images resonate and reflect upon the shape of the world as we perceive it—they can enlarge its possibilities and increase our freedom to respond to the call of God that lies behind and in the specific images of the biblical texts as God's call also lies (often hidden) behind the images that seem natural to us because they are part of our world.

Two great themes come together in this chapter—the resurrection of Christ and the hope of the believer that our work (through which God in Christ has worked) is "not in vain."

Paul's bold faith that the appearance of Christ to him, Paul, was of the same nature and validity as the foundational appearances to Peter and the twelve can be a liberating insight to us. It was by finding life transformed, given new direction and energy by the encounter with Christ, that Paul and the other early believers were assured of Christ's living presence. Thus, there is a very close connection between the continuing experience of the Spirit of Christ in the ongoing life of the community, and the foundational appearances to the apostles. It was around these experiences and this sense of the transformation of life that the fuller, no doubt partly legendary, narratives of the resurrection in the Gospels arose.

How can we speak of this presence? Two aspects are central: awareness that God has drawn near, and recognizing a connection between the story of Jesus and this fresh sense of God's nearness. "God has drawn near" means especially that God did not forget Jesus. It was a fresh sense of the presence of God that made both the experience of the resurrection and that of Christ at work in the community so important and transforming. The experience of generations of Christians has been that the story of Jesus' life and death freshly opens us to the awareness of God's being very near.

The pattern of imagination in which Paul and others responded to their encounter with the nearness of God was the pattern of a future resurrection brought into the present. It was a matter of course to them that their experience included not only an awareness of God but also an awareness of the renewed presence of the Jesus whose story they knew. They thought of Jesus as renewed to life and encountering them, and this is still a valid interpretation of the resurrection. But it is equally valid to say that the fusion of a new sense of God's presence with the memories of Jesus was a combination that made the appearances possible, so that what was actually living in the experiences was God's presence. Jesus lived in the perception of this presence in the sense that memories of Jesus shaped it and made it accessible, and thus what he had begun was carried forward among those who experienced the resurrection. The two views are not as different as they seem at first sight, for in both cases the heart of the experience is the confidence and joy that spring from a new sense that God is near as a transforming power, a closeness brought into our lives by our meeting with the story of Jesus.

2. The Hope for a Future Life

As we address the complex, intense, and often difficult vision of the future in this text, a similar openness to a variety of interpretations is necessary if we are to do justice to it. The reason why such openness to variety is important is that if we insist on one particular interpretation, we may restrict the deep interaction of the biblical story with our daily patterns of life and belief, in which so much of Paul's vision is problematic. Paul's vision of hope can only deeply encounter ours if we are free to let both the world of the text and our world speak. Let us consider five of these problematic aspects of the text.

First, Paul believed that the end was near. He says, "we will not all die" (verse 51), because he expected that some of those to whom he wrote would still be alive at the end (see also 7:29–31). For him the nearness of the end was a positive, liberating aspect of faith, and one that energized him to action. Today we do not expect the end of life on earth to be the climax of God's purpose, but rather the result of a drastic abuse of human power or of the exhaustion of the earth's resources. We cannot copy Paul. But we can find our faith renewed by the sense of God's nearness and transforming power that Paul expressed in this image.

The hope for the end brought a profound freedom in social behavior and role patterns. Such freedom could be abused, and how to exercise it was a major subject of discussion between Paul and the Corinthians, as we have seen. It is clear that many in Corinth rejoiced in their freedom to take new roles in the church and family, as we see most clearly from the claims of new roles for women. Some may have turned to inward faith, but both Paul and many others saw that accepted patterns of life could be changed, and could envision new structures that could better express the fullness of life that God intends not only for the few but for all. Finding new ways of living together was the great mark of the faith that the end was near.

New lifestyles and new commitments that will be forces for change both in the church and in the wider society are a major part of the call of God as we hear it today. The growing gap between the rich and the poor, an economy that creates a large urban underclass, the continuing privilege of the few and prejudice against those who are perceived as different, and the abuse of the earth's resources are all marks of the world that people of faith are called to confront and challenge, to live against "as if not" (7:29–31), as both Paul and many in Corinth did in their day. As we interpret the resurrection faith, we must turn it in such a this-worldly direction if we are to be faithful to this chapter.

Second, to Paul it was essential that the future would come in the form of a new kind of "body," although he strongly repudiated a literal "flesh and blood" vision of the resurrection. A great deal of theological effort has been expended in maintaining the distinction between "resurrection of the body" and "immortality of the soul." This effort has been helpful in pointing to those aspects of the "body" that made the term so important to Paul. The body, both the present one and that which is to come, are gifts of God and not intrinsic possessions. The body symbolizes the whole person, rather than the powerless, ghostly survival in which many ancient people believed. The body is the instrument of communication, which enables life to be in community. These are basic insights. But we need to go beyond the separation between body and spirit or soul that makes it necessary to insist on the resurrection of the body. If we are to imagine our own existence freshly, and find in it the openness to God's action that animates Paul's vision, it may be more important for us to focus on Paul's conviction that "flesh and blood cannot inherit the kingdom of God" (15:50). To us, "body" has become so intimately associated with "flesh and blood" that other images may better help us to understand that our frail and temporary existences may truly contribute to God's existence. We could not hope for a future life except on the basis of an intimate communion with God. If soul and body are not different kinds of substance, but different in degree, we may think of both of them as continuing flows of experience. Then we may express our hope in symbols drawn from either side of our present makeup.

Third, it was an unreflective assumption for Paul that in the end God would win out completely. God would be "all in all" (15:28). This was a generally accepted image that lay in the background of the chapter. In most such visions of the future, God's total victory is possible because most of humanity—those who do not fit the picture of God's triumph—are consigned to destruction. First Corinthians 15 bypasses this aspect of the final triumph, as we have seen, and concentrates only on those who belong to Christ. Thus in the text there is a move toward greater openness than was common in such visions. But Paul still assumed that God would compel history to come out in a certain way. Hence the deeper issue is, "Is it right to assume that God, in the end, will act by force?" That kind of action is presupposed by any image of God's total victory. Yet much in the Bible, and very much in Paul, goes in a different direction, and offers us images of God as persuading human beings (and all the creation), as struggling with the world, as suffering with it, as caring. These images cannot be reconciled with the image of a God who forces a certain final conclusion on history.

Thus, though the image of a final victory does indeed provide the structure of Paul's narrative of the end, the content he gives to the story is very different from the traditional one, especially in his neglecting the theme of final judgment. As we read this chapter, many will find that its emphasis on redemption requires us to rethink and restructure our vision of how God acts and will act, to picture an open story, one in which God "improvises" in response to and in struggle with human beings and with the whole creation—a story that is genuinely open and not directed to a predetermined goal. Of course, that will mean that God's reception of our lives into God's existence will be seen not as something that takes place at a final end, but step-by-step as the generations pass.

Here we may also mention the intimate link that Paul saw between the final consummation of all existence and the motivation for doing what is good and right. Especially in 1 Corinthians 15:12–19, 29–34, it is strongly said that there would be no point in doing right unless we could hope for the final completion of all existence in the coming resurrection. ("If for this life only we have hoped in Christ, we are of all people most to be pitied" [verse 19]). Along with his firm faith that through Christ we are accepted by God in spite of our sins, Paul also held that we would be judged and rewarded. But this hope was not focused on an image of balancing the books, despite the way in which this aspect of reward is sometimes accented to make the point that our actions really matter. What lies behind the image of future reward for Paul is his faith that all the details of our lives will find their fulfillment in the final fulfillment of God's will. (See the treatment of this theme in Victor P. Furnish, *Theology and Ethics in Paul*, 115–135.) The hope that all our existence is taken up and transformed in God can also be affirmed in the open story of God's encounter with the world that is suggested above.

Fourth, how are we to respond to the way in which Paul focuses all perception of God's presence on the figure of Christ, a focus expressed in this chapter by God's delegating authority to Christ until all opposing powers have been destroyed (15:20–28)? Paul knew very well that many of the ingredients of his faith were well established long before the time of Jesus, as is shown, for instance, by his quotations of scripture. But for him these ingredients had been recombined, so to speak, in such a way that all the elements of faith, even so general an element as a sense of right and wrong, could not function rightly except in the field of force that was Christ. We can affirm the same, but we will have to do so with a wider appreciation of the work of the Spirit of Christ beyond the margins of the biblical story or the story of our faith, and in particular with a renewed appreciation of the way in which the call of Christ is not a call to hold fast to what has already been formulated, but a call to transform our world by incorporating into it images and patterns of relationship that have been developed in other traditions. Much in Paul already points to Christ as a power of transformation, and this theme must be central in our appropriation of his faith.

Finally, what about life after death, the explicit theme of the chapter? Paul and other early Christians were able to picture the renewed presence of Christ as a resurrection because they already believed in a future resurrection, and thus they understood the presence of Christ as a first step in the general resurrection that they already believed in. Much Christian thinking has reversed this relationship, and made the resurrection of Christ the starting point for understanding the future—indeed this process of reversal is already under way in 1 Corinthians 15.

Here, too, we need to be careful not to insist too quickly on a "literal translation" of Paul's vision. What links the two parts of chapter 15 is this deep conviction: God remembered Jesus; God will remember us. How that remembering took place and will take place was expressed in the form of the resurrection of a transformed body. But the animating faith was that we are not forgotten.

There is room for more than one way of expressing how we are remembered by God: some will hold that only the biblical story gives any clue to our hope; they will emphasize the "alien" character of Christian faith in a world that is forgetting its Christian roots, or never really had such roots. For these, the resurrection of the body can be affirmed whether or not anything in the wider world supports it. This voice needs to be heard, but if it becomes the dominant one, we may fail to see the work of God outside our tradition, and in this pluralistic world we cannot afford to withdraw from this interaction with all of God's work.

Others will look in the biblical tradition, but also to the wider creation for signs of the trustworthiness of God. Though the specific focus of hope is to be found in the biblical story as reinterpreted in the church, the whole of creation also reinforces this vision. Such a theology of creation has usually been a central strand of Christian thinking. It has been thrown into question for many today because the world is so chaotic. We believe that a new image of God as persuasive, rather than as coercive, as suggested above, can renew this traditional way of linking the insights of our specific tradition to our wider experience. This way of thinking will be open both to the biblical image of resurrection and to images such as the immortality of the soul to open our imagination to the future. The character of God as known in our tradition and in our wider experience will be the ground of hope for the future, not a special knowledge of what the future will be like. The image of resurrection will be taken seriously but not literally, and what the future will be like will be left for the future to reveal.

Still others will stand in the Christian tradition, but will not privilege the resurrection narratives as they look to the future. They will look to the whole gamut of experience, religious and not explicitly religious, for evidence, as is shown in the lively recent interest in near-death experiences. Often rejected out of hand as "New Age," this perspective may help many to break down too narrow a view of what is possible in the spiritual life.

Though this writer is closest to the second of these options, grounding hope in a theology of creation, it is important to recognize both the value of the one-sided concentration on the biblical story only, and also the value of the wider view that searches all sorts of experience.

Some will dislike this suggested openness, claiming that we need to find some definite and clear belief about life after death. On the contrary, since our hope is that God will not forget us—a theme basic to this chapter—we may leave the details to God. Some will affirm that being remembered by God is sufficient, that our contribution to life will make a permanent difference in God's experience. Others, like the present writer, will affirm that the spontaneity of personal life will continue in God's presence, but will not try to imagine what this will be like. Others will try to develop images of what a continuing growth of a human being in another life can be. Any of these ways can be an affirmation that our life and actions are not in vain.

Such openness to more than one possible way of thinking about the future, though different from the way in which Paul sketched out what he believed, is profoundly in keeping with a central Pauline theme, that we live not by holding fast to what we have, but by letting go.

16:1–24

The Collection, Travel Plans, Exhortations, and Greetings

The final chapter of 1 Corinthians brings together a varied collection of materials. Some details are not clear to us, though no doubt they were clear enough to the recipients of the letter. The rather miscellaneous nature of this chapter has led some students of Paul to conclude that parts of it were originally written separately for different occasions and later put together by an editor. (See the Introduction, pp. 15–18, for the question whether 1 Corinthians is a unity.) But the final section of a Pauline letter often brings together various scattered points that Paul finds still need to be made, and there is no need to parcel out this chapter between different supposed original sources.

16:1–4 The Collection

The instructions about how to raise money for the church in Jerusalem begin with the phrase, "Now concerning...." The "concerning" may indicate that the question of the collection had been raised by the Corinthians in their letter to Paul. (See 7:1, "Now concerning the matters about which you wrote....") But the repetition of the phrase may be by chance, and the subject of the collection may well come up simply because it was an important final point for Paul.

Paul's directions for gathering the contribution show that Sunday ("the first day of every week," verse 2) was already a special day of Christian worship, and thus that the seven-day week, taken from Jewish practice, was also part of the pattern of the life of the Christian congregation. But the accumulation of money is to take place weekly in each home, not in the church (which, of course, did not have a special building). When Paul comes it will all be gathered together. We know from 2 Corinthians 8 and 9 that a good deal of further planning was required before this gift was completed, but eventually it became part of the offering to Jerusalem recounted in Acts (see Acts 24:17; compare also Romans 15:24–33)—though no messengers from Corinth are mentioned in Acts in the list of those who accompanied Paul (Acts 20:4).

Some interpreters have regarded this contribution as a kind of church tax, similar to a tax paid annually by practicing Jews for the temple in Jerusalem. If so, this offering would be a forerunner of the money later collected regularly by the church at Rome, when it had become a center of the church, just as Jerusalem was the center at this early period. But the gift planned by Paul was not a regular annual contribution like a tax. It was a one-time gift. Jerusalem did have a special place, suggested here by calling the Christians in Jerusalem simply "the saints" or believers, without even mentioning the city by name. But as is clearly stated here and also in 2 Corinthians 8 and 9, this was no tax, but a free gift. In Galatians 2:10 Paul recounts that the leaders in Jerusalem had asked that the Gentile believers "remember the poor," and in Romans 15:26 he specifically notes that the offering was being accumulated for "the poor among the saints in Jerusalem." It was not a case of "the poor" being a term for the "pious." There is little doubt that Paul saw this gift as a way of increasing the solidarity between the very different congregations in Jerusalem and Corinth.

At any rate, the passage shows how little organized the economic practices of the church were as yet.

16:5–9 Paul's Travel Plans

Paul plans to come soon; he must go to Macedonia first. When he comes, he wants to be able to spend some time. He has not yet decided where to go after that (see also verse 4 above, where it is an open question whether he will go with the group who carry the offering to Jerusalem). We learn from 2 Corinthians that the actual course of events led to more than one future visit, and was difficult for Paul. Especially noteworthy is the concluding sentence: he will stay at Ephesus until Pentecost (late spring) because "a wide door for effective work has opened to me, and there are many adversaries" (verse 9). Work

159

for Paul typically takes place in the face of opposition, but he seems to face this with a certain relish in spite of the uncertainty of the results in any specific case. This passing comment casts light on the "not in vain" theme of chapter 15.

16:10–12 Timothy and Apollos

Timothy was apparently already on his way (4:17). The "if" in verse 10 does not indicate any doubt that he would actually get there; as in English, the Greek term is often closer to "when." Paul had some question about how well Timothy would be received. Whom Paul expected to come with Timothy when he returned to Ephesus we do not know.

As for Apollos (verse 12), it is not clear why he did not go to Corinth when Paul urged him. "He [Apollos] was not at all willing to come now" (NRSV) may mean "it was not at all God's will for him to come now" (NRSV footnote). This brief note about Apollos does not give any indication that there was a break between Paul and Apollos, although in Corinth some set the one against the other. (See above on 1:12; 3:4–9; 4:6.)

16:13–18 Exhortations and Commendations

Verse 13 is made up of traditional and very general ethical exhortations, which are quite appropriate at the close of a letter. The first term, "keep alert" (or "watch"), comes from the vocabulary of hope for the end.

Then follows a commendation of Stephanas and his household as leaders; Paul evidently doubted that everyone would be willing to accept this leadership. Just as the plans for the collection show how fluid the economic base of the community was, the reference to Stephanas and his household shows how fluid the leadership roles still were. No doubt the rank of Stephanas and his household was partly given by their relative affluence, but also their being "the first converts in Achaia" also contributed (verse 15; Achaia was the province in which Corinth was situated).

A tiny glimpse into the growth of forms of leadership is offered by Paul's comment, "they have devoted themselves to the service of the saints" (verse 15). The term "service" is from the same stem as the word for servant, which soon came to be a technical term, "deacon." But as yet there is no definite position, only voluntary service. See below on the tension between the emerging leadership and the vision of an open community.

Stephanas, Fortunatus, and Achaicus were one of Paul's sources of information about the church at Corinth.

16:19–20 Greetings

Paul's letters often include greetings at the close. It is worth noting that Apollos does not send greetings; perhaps he was away from Ephesus at the moment. Aquila and Prisca, who were now established in Ephesus sufficiently for them to have a "church in their house" (verse 19), had come there from Corinth, where they had taken refuge when expelled with other Jews from Rome, according to Acts 18:2. Paul sends greetings to them in Romans 16:3, a chapter that some scholars believe was directed not to Rome but to Ephesus.

The "holy kiss" was already a liturgical act. It may be mentioned here because Paul expected his letter to be read in a meeting of the congregation; at this point, at the end, they would exchange the ceremonial kiss.

16:21–24 Closing

The closing words may well be liturgical as well, but before he turns to them Paul adds a greeting in his own handwriting, as in Galatians 6:11. The rest of the letter had been dictated to a secretary.

The striking curse on anyone who does not love the Lord (verse 22) may well be a quotation by Paul from a liturgical phrase. It uses a Greek word for "love" (*phileo*) that does not appear elsewhere in Paul's writing. It is possible that it was a statement that was intended to exclude nonbelievers from the Lord's Supper. Surely the following cry, "Our Lord, come!" was a liturgical cry. It may also be translated, "Our Lord has come!" but the cry for the coming of the Lord is more probable. (Both the curse and the call for the Lord to come are Aramaic words, not Greek.) We know little about the details of their use.

Preaching and Teaching on 1 Corinthians 16

Two items in the chapter are worth comment. One, of course, is the "collection," for contributions of money are still so great a preoccupation of the church. We must remember, however, that this collection was in no way intended for use in Corinth.

161

It reminds us that from the beginning of the church, congregations of very different kinds have needed and do need each other. And Paul was making an important point when he planned that the money would not simply be sent, but that some people from the Corinthian church would go to Jerusalem. Differences between suburban and inner-city congregations provide an opportunity in our own time to explore the kind of interchange between different sorts of Christians that is intended by the collection. Now, as then, each kind has rich gifts to offer to a different style of congregation, as Paul pointed out in connection with this in Romans 15:27. We may regard the building of contacts among very different congregations as a major challenge for the church today.

The other matter worth pondering is the tension between the open community, in which very different kinds of people interact, and the emerging leadership that Paul mentions in verses 15–18. As time passed, most parts of the church have become far more dependent on established and even bureaucratic leadership, and this is as true of the "free" churches as it is of those with explicitly hierarchical forms of ministry. No continuing organization can exist across time without some form of recognized leadership. How to establish this, and at the same time remain open to the spontaneity that we glimpse in the Corinthian congregation, is a major issue for churches to study and ponder. If we had more faith in the presence of the Spirit we might be able to deal with this tension more profoundly.

Works Cited

(For a note on how these books were selected, see the Preface, pp.vii-viii. Page citations are to references to the book in this commentary.)

Barrett, C. K., *A Commentary on the First Epistle to the Corinthians* (New York, Harper and Row, 1968). p. 50
A fine commentary in traditional format.

Beardslee, William A., *Human Achievement and Divine Vocation in the Message of Paul* (Naperville, Illinois: Alec R. Allenson, 1961). p. 45
A book that works to overcome the gap between faith and "works."

Boswell, John, *Christianity, Social Tolerance, and Homosexuality* (Chicago: University of Chicago Press, 1980). pp. 58-59
A pathbreaking work in showing that attitudes toward homosexuality in the church have been far more flexible than we have traditionally thought. Yet in his discussion of Paul's words in chapter 6, Boswell goes too far in claiming that there is no reference there to homosexuality.

Braun, Herbert, *Jesus of Nazareth: The Man and His Time* (Philadelphia: Fortress, 1979). p. 69
Still worth reading along with the many more recent books on Jesus.

163

1 CORINTHIANS

Castelli, Elizabeth, *Imitating Paul: A Discourse of Power* (Louis-ville: Westminster/John Knox, 1991). pp. 45, 99
Using an analysis partly derived from the French thinker Michel Foucault, this book uncovers the element of effort to control and establish uniformity in Paul's advice that people imitate him. A valuable insight, but one that needs to be balanced by other strands in Paul's thought that are interactive and open to diversity.

Conzelmann, Hans, *A Commentary on the First Epistle to the Corinthians*, trans. James W. Leitch (Philadelphia: Fortress Press, 1975). pp. 50, 95, 122
Indispensable for its scope of information, this solid com-mentary is limited by its rigid theological framework for interpretation.

Doty, William G., *Letters in Primitive Christianity* (Philadelphia: Fortress, 1973). p. 8
A useful introduction to the functions of ancient Christian letters.

Epperly, Bruce G., *At the Edges of Life: A Holistic Vision of the Human Adventure* (St. Louis: Chalice Press, 1992). p. 113
With wisdom and imagination, this book introduces a wide spectrum of New Age spiritual practices from a Christian point of view.

Funk, Robert W., *Language, Hermeneutic, and Word of God* (New York: Harper & Row, 1964). p. 10
A pioneer work in contemporary interpretation theory; the section on Paul's letters is very perceptive about the inter-play of form and content.

Furnish, Victor Paul, *The Moral Teaching of Paul* (Nashville: Abingdon Press, 1979). pp. 60, 67
A fine work for helping Paul speak to our moral concerns.

Furnish, Victor Paul, *Theology and Ethics in Paul* (Nashville: Abingdon Press, 1978). p. 155
A more thorough work than the above, this is a classic exploration of the subject of its title.

Knox, John, *Chapters in a Life of Paul* (New York: Abingdon-Cokesbury, 1950). p. 35
An insightful portrayal of many aspects of Paul.

Kuck, David W., *Judgment and Community Conflict: Paul's Use of Apocalyptic Judgment Language in 1 Corinthians 3:5—4:5* (Leiden: E. J. Brill, 1991). p. 143
Kuck relates the rhetoric about judgment in 1 Corinthians to Paul's pastoral concerns, showing Paul's concern for variety in the community.

Meeks, Wayne A., *The First Urban Christians: The Social World of the Apostle Paul* (New Haven: Yale University: 1983). pp. 4, 27
Very important for its probing of the social function of early Christian practices and beliefs; much about Corinth.

Polk, David P., editor, *Now What's a Christian to Do?* (St. Louis: Chalice Press, 1994). p. 77
The chapters focus discussion on six contemporary issues from the point of view of Christian process theology. The chapter on teenage spirituality and sexuality complements the discussion in this book by approaching the interplay between the Bible and our world from the contemporary end.

Scroggs, Robin, *The New Testament and Homosexuality* (Philadelphia: Fortress, 1983). p. 59
Shows that we cannot simply follow the New Testament statements literally.

Schüssler Fiorenza, Elisabeth, *In Memory of Her: A Feminist Theological Reconstruction of Christian Origins* (New York: Crossroad, 1983). p. 138
A pioneer work in bringing to light the central role of women in early Christianity, a role that was often over-looked or concealed in the texts. The author sees Paul as supporting the Corinthian women prophets, while at the same time, for the purpose of maintaining orderly proce-dure, trying to set limits that were later developed in ways that were repressive to women.

Schweitzer, Albert, *The Mysticism of Paul the Apostle,* trans. William Montgomery (London: A. & C. Black, 1931). p. 44
An imaginative picture of Paul's "eschatological mysti-cism."

1 CORINTHIANS

Talbert, Charles H., *Reading Corinthians: A Literary and Theological Commentary on I and II Corinthians* (New York: Crossroad, 1987).pp. 2, 109
Concentrates on the literary structure and on how the structure illuminates the meaning.

Wire, Antoinette Clark, *The Corinthian Women Prophets: A Reconstruction Through Paul's Rhetoric* (Minneapolis: Fortress, 1990). p. 137
A very thorough study of how Paul's rhetoric reflects positions that he was opposing, mainly the positions of women prophets. A valuable study, though the method of constructing a picture of the women prophets by finding what Paul was "opposing" highlights the elements of conflict between Paul and the church in Corinth, and portrays him as more legalistic than he appears in the intepretation offered here.

Index of Principal Themes

Baptism	24, 58, 70, 93, 116
Biblical interpretation, Paul's	89-90, 92-94, 106
Boasting	27, 32-33, 44, 91
Body	60-61, 62
as image	116–17
resurrection of the body: *see* Resurrection	
Christ	*passim* and 52, 88, 94, 110-115, 120-21
cross of Christ	35, 40-42, 120
Church: *see* Community, Christian	
Community, Christian	
as field of force	50, 55-56, 57-58
as judge	49-51, 57
boundaries of	53, 58-59, 61, 75-76, 82, 87, 94, 97-98, 100, 101-102
building up the community	62, 98, 133-34, 140, 150
defilement of	47-56
divisions in	22-25, 108-11
leadership in	30-32, 88, 160, 162
see also: Paul, as apostle	
Lord's Supper in: *see* Lord's Supper	
money collected in	158-59, 162
openness to variety in	17, 25, 45, 59-60, 100, 111-112, 115
social makeup of	4, 27, 86, 109, 117
Divorce: *see* Marriage	
End of world: *see* Nearness of the End	
Endurance	95
Faith	10-11, 13-15, 70, 115, 125
Food	46, 60, 80-81, 87-88, 93-94, 97-98
see also: Lord's Supper	
Freedom	7-8, 12-13, 98-99
God	*passim* and 83-85, 148-49
Homosexuality	58-60
Idolatry	83-86
Judgment, Last	31, 34-35, 51, 57, 95, 146, 154
Knowledge, and love	83-86
Letter form and outline of 1 Corinthians	6-9
Lord's Supper	93-94, 95-97, 108-14
Love	13-15, 67, 77, 98-99, 121-33
and knowledge	83-86
and self-consciousness	13-15
asymmetry of giving	33
of God	83-84

1 CORINTHIANS

Marriage   62-78
   and celibacy   66, 68-69
   divorce   69-70
   equality in   66-68, 74-75, 78
   sexual relations in   65-67
   unimportance of   63, 76
   with nonbelievers   70

Men, appearance of   106

Nearness of the End   73, 111, 152

"New Age" spirituality   14, 111, 156

Occasion for 1 Corinthians   4-6

Other faiths   16, 26, 84-85, 101-02

Paul   *passim*
   as apostle   42-45, 80, 86-92, 99-100, 118, 144-45
   claim to authority   7, 28, 30-31, 32-34, 86-92, 99-100
   did not always answer questions directly   7, 64, 83

Power, powers   26-27, 31-32, 48-50, 81-86, 94, 97
   in liturgical acts   94, 97, 109-10, 112-13
   of apostle: *see* Paul, as apostle

Radical transformation and continuing responsibility   11-13

Resolution and tension   34-36, 37

Resurrection   130, 143-157
   interpretation of   150-57
   of believers   145-50, 152-57
   of Christ   144-45, 150-52

Speaking in tongues   115, 118, 124, 133-37, 140-42

Spirit   3, 28-29, 31, 36-38, 60, 100-01, 114-21
   as field of force   114-15, 119-20
   gifts of   114-16, 118-19, 127-28, 133, 140-42

Transformation and responsibility   11-15, 65, 78, 117-18, 121

Wisdom   26-29, 38-40, 83, 106-08, 122-23, 148

Women
   appearance of   104-08
   as leaders   22-23, 68, 137-38, 142, 152
   speaking in worship   104-05, 137-40, 141